BANQUETS & BEGGARS

W. A. POOVEY

DRAMAS AND MEDITATIONS
ON SIX PARABLES

AUGSBURG PUBLISHING HOUSE
MINNEAPOLIS, MINNESOTA

BANQUETS AND BEGGARS

The dramas in this book are also available in a separate
volume, *Banquets and Beggars: Dramas on Six Parables*.
No performance fee is required providing a copy of the
play is purchased for each player.

Contents

Preface

The parables of Jesus never seem to lose their appeal for Christians. In every age the parables have been reinterpreted to speak to the needs of the time. It may or may not be true that one picture is better than a thousand words, but these little pictures painted by Jesus have a fascination and a timeliness about them that never grows dim.

Just because they are stories, pictures, images, the parables also suggest dramas. They invite us to illustrate the wider implications of Jesus' words or to seek to illumine their meaning by describing specific situations to which the message of the parable can be applied. The plays in this book represent an effort to emphasize some aspect of a parable or to reset the story in a modern frame.

The choice of parables here is not intended to suggest that these particular passages are Advent, Christmas or Epiphany oriented. Indeed each play could be presented at any time during the church year. Yet, because the opening Sundays of the church calendar focus on many of the great truths of Christianity, the plays in this book can speak specifically to the Advent, Christmas, Epiphany season.

The message that follows each play is intended to suggest *a* line of approach. It is not intended as a *must* interpretation and each minister should choose his own approach to parable and play. The seasonal emphasis is placed at the end of each meditation, not woven in the main discourse. This allows for flexibility if the material is used at a different time in the church year.

Increasingly modern church worship seeks greater participation by lay members in the service. While the material in this book does not have to be limited to Sunday morning worship, the dramas offer another outlet for lay participation in the work of the church.

No drama or meditation can equal the artistry of the parable itself as spoken by our Lord. But if the material here presented helps to make us appreciate a little more the truth of Jesus' message, the book will have served its purpose.

Production Notes

The plays make simple demands for scenery, costumes, and stagecraft. Every church building and parish hall is different from all others and so the actual adaption of the play to the local situation rests with the ingenuity of director and actors.

The plays are most effective of course when presented by a capable and well-rehearsed cast. Most congregations have more people with dramatic ability or latent talent than they imagine. However, because the plays are simple and the action not too involved, it is possible to present the dramas by a reading production. Even a reading performance should be carefully rehearsed, however.

Where desirable, congregations may form a circuit with each church preparing one or more plays and then shifting in rotation. There is no particular sequence that must be followed as far as the plays are concerned.

Whether to use a meditation with each play depends on local circumstances. If a meditation is not used it may be wise to provide a time for discussion and reflection. Dramas are not a teaching medium in themselves but are intended to evoke a mood or to stir thinking. So some followup may prove useful although not absolutely necessary.

The Great Feast

Luke 14:15-24
FIRST SUNDAY IN ADVENT

DRAMA	**Excuses! Excuses!**
MEDITATION	**Come Feast with Me**

Excuses! Excuses!

Based on Luke 14:15-24. The parable may be read before
the play but this is not necessary.

CHARACTERS

LAMAL: spokesman for the group, smooth and oily

HAVER: wily, sharp, and inclined to lose temper

BENET: the idiot, stupid and honest

NATHAN: the giver of the feast; noble, fair-minded but
firm

MARCUS: the servant, polite but unruffled by others

LYDA: an old woman, small, dirty but happy-looking; no
lines to speak

KEM: young boy, ragged but smiling; no lines to speak

GARDIS: an old man, lame but cheerful; no lines to speak

SETTING

Bare stage. A chair will be placed almost in center as play
proceeds.

COSTUMES

The play may be played in typical Palestinian robes or in
modern dress as desired.

8

(As scene opens, LAMAL, HAVER, and BENET advance to the center of the stage and speak to the audience. The rhyming lines should be spoken in a rather stilted manner, like the recitation of a small child.)

LAMAL: We are the men who made excuses.

HAVER: We tried to explain—

BENET: No use—

ALL: No use.

LAMAL: He said that I was a terrible sinner
    Because I didn't turn up for his dinner.

BENET: My wife said, "Don't go."

HAVER: My oxen seemed slow.

LAMAL: My land deal came through,—
    Now what would you do?

ALL: So we all made excuses and missed the feast—

BENET: And now we're in trouble . . .

HAVER: *(Interrupting.)* That's enough silly rhyming. Let's tell these people what it's all about. Lamal, you're the spokesman. Explain our situation to everybody here.

LAMAL: All right. *(To audience again.)* You see, good people, we're the three men in the parable of the Great Feast. We were invited to dinner at Nathan's house but we didn't go because—well—because we thought we had more important things to do. And that made Nathan very angry.

BENET: *(Cutting in.)* And he had a right to be angry. We shouldn't have broken our promise after we said we'd come.

HAVER: *(Impatiently.)* Be quiet, Benet. We don't need any of your preaching. If you feel that way about it, you should have stayed home.

BENET: But I was only trying to tell everybody the truth.

HAVER: Some truth is better left unsaid. Go on, Lamal.

LAMAL: There's not much more to tell. *(To audience.)* Nathan has refused to invite us to his home again.

BENET: And that's too bad because he does give good feasts.

HAVER: *(Angry.)* Will you be quiet! *(Slyly.)* It's Nathan's friendship we miss, not his feasts. Keep that in mind when we talk to him. *(Aside.)* Idiot!

BENET: *(Almost in tears.)* I was only—

LAMAL: We know, we know. *(To audience.)* You see, my friends, Nathan is giving another feast tonight and we're not invited. But we're here anyway, hoping he'll change his mind when he sees us. He's inclined to be a bit tender-hearted.

HAVER: *(Laughing.)* What you mean is that he's a soft-headed fool. *(To audience.)* People are always taking advantage of Nathan and he never realizes it. He thinks he's being *(mocking)* fair and just to everyone. So, if we can play on his sympathy a bit and also make him feel that he was unfair to us—

BENET: *(Interrupting.)* Which of course he wasn't. We deserved—(HAVER and LAMAL *put their hands over* BENET's *mouth as he struggles to continue.*)

HAVER: *(Fiercely.)* Will you be quiet? (BENET *nods.*) All right. *(They release him.)*

LAMAL: Such an idiot!

BENET: I was only—*(They advance on him again.* BENET *puts his hand over his own mouth.)*

HAVER: Enough explanations. Let's see if Nathan will come and talk to us. Lamal, call him.

LAMAL: All right. *(Calls.)* Nathan! *Nathan!* NATHAN! *(Silence.)*

BENET: *(Timidly.)* Maybe he's asleep.

HAVER: *(Scornfully.)* At his own feast? We'll all have to call. *(All three shout loudly for* NATHAN *who finally appears.)*

NATHAN: What's all this noise about? *(Recognizes them.)* Oh, it's you three, Lamal, Haver, and Benet. You were told that I never wanted to see you again. Go away and don't bother me. *(Starts to go in again.)*

HAVER: Wait. Wait, Nathan. You're not being fair.

NATHAN: *(Stung.)* Not being fair! I like that. I invited you three to a feast and you all accepted. But when Marcus came to tell you everything was ready, you each gave him a flimsy excuse. That was an insult to me and you know it. How dare you say I'm not being fair!

BENET: *(To others.)* He's right, you know. We *did* insult him.

HAVER: *(In loud whisper.)* Benet, shut up if you value your health. *(To Nathan, sweetly.)* I understand how you feel, Nathan. But there were circumstances—

LAMAL: At least you ought to listen to our stories—

BENET: Then you can have us thrown out, if you want to.

HAVER: *(Aside.)* Imbecile!

NATHAN: All right, all right. My guests are busy eating, so I suppose I can waste a few minutes listening to your lame excuses. But I'm going to have Marcus present so you don't try to fill my ears with lies. *(Calling.)* Marcus. Marcus.

MARCUS: *(Appearing in doorway.)* Yes sir.

NATHAN: Bring me a chair and then stand beside me while we listen to these three *former* friends.

MARCUS: Yes sir. *(Goes offstage.)*

NATHAN: This is against my better judgment but I suppose it can't do any harm. I warn you though. Be brief and truthful or you'll regret it.

LAMAL: You can count on us, Nathan.

NATHAN: I once thought I could.

BENET: He caught you there, Lamal. (LAMAL *glares at him.)*

MARCUS: *(Reappearing.)* Here's your chair, sir.

NATHAN: Good, put it right here in the center so I can preside like a judge. (MARCUS *places chair near center and* NATHAN *sits on it.* BENET, LAMAL, *and* HAVER *are on one side of the stage,* MARCUS *on the other.)* Now Marcus, stand beside me and tell me about your visits to Lamal.

MARCUS: Yes sir. I gave him your invitation to the feast a week ahead of time. He seemed pleased to be invited and assured me that he would come. But when I went to tell him everything was ready he seemed—different.

NATHAN: Different? In what way?

MARCUS: Well, first he pretended that I had told him the wrong day. When I wouldn't agree, he got very huffy and said he wasn't coming to the feast anyway. And when I asked what I should tell you, he finally admitted that he had bought some property and wanted to go and see it. I came back after that and reported his excuse to you.

NATHAN: Thank you, Marcus. Anything wrong with that story, Lamal?

LAMAL: No, Nathan. That's the way it happened all right.

NATHAN: Then what's your complaint?

LAMAL: I'm not complaining. I only want to tell you about that piece of property.

NATHAN: All right, if you must.

LAMAL: Nathan, have you ever wanted anything so much that you would almost die to get it?

NATHAN: I suppose so.

LAMAL: That's the way I felt about the property I bought. All my life I've wanted some land along the lake. There's something about water that pleases and soothes me. I love to hear waves lap against the shore, and big breakers pound against the rocks. I love the breeze when it comes off the water. I love—but I won't bore you with my feelings. It's enough that I wanted land by the lake, particularly the stretch of shore just opposite the tiny island they call Golan. I wanted that property the way Ahab wanted Naboth's vineyard.

NATHAN: In other words, you coveted another man's property.

LAMAL: Coveting is a hard word but I'll accept it if it makes you understand how I felt. And on the very day of your feast old Zacchee offered to sell me the spot that I wanted. I bought it immediately and that's why I didn't show up for your banquet.

NATHAN: You couldn't wait one day? Even to keep your promise to me, your friend?

LAMAL: Nothing would have kept me from that property. For the moment, it was the most important thing in the world for me.

NATHAN: I see. Well, that's about what I expected.

LAMAL: Do try to understand.

NATHAN: Let me hear the others before making any comment. Haver, you're next. But first, Marcus?

MARCUS: Well, sir, Haver was just like Lamal. He

was glad for the invitation when I first asked him. But when I went back, he even refused to open the door to me. He yelled and told me to go away. Then he mumbled that he had to go and test some oxen he'd bought and I wasn't to bother him. So I came back and reported to you.

NATHAN: Anything to add, Haver?

HAVER: No, Marcus is telling the truth. But I was angry and upset that day.

NATHAN: At me? Or at Marcus?

HAVER: Oh no. But I don't like being cheated. Nobody gets the better of Haver. That's always been my boast. But after I bought those oxen somebody told me that the oxen were old and lame. And that made me see red.

NATHAN: So red that you couldn't come to my dinner?

HAVER: So red that I couldn't think of anything else except getting even with the man who had cheated me. I'd have been a terrible guest at a feast, so I didn't come. That's the whole story. Except that the rumor was false and the oxen were actually all right.

NATHAN: Hearing your side of the story doesn't excite my sympathy very much. But now Benet, let's see what you have to say.

BENET: You don't need to question Marcus. I won't deny whatever he has to say. But Nathan, I had just gotten married and that made everything very difficult.

NATHAN: I don't see why. I invited you to bring your wife along.

BENET: I know you did, Nathan. Very kind, very kind. But I'll never understand women, I'm afraid. She planned to come and then she decided she didn't have anything to wear and she told me to go without her. And when I got ready to go, she cried. So when Marcus came I was all flustered and said the first thing that came into my mind.

MARCUS: He slammed the door in my face, sir.

BENET: Yes, I know I did. Afterwards I was sorry. But she told me to do it. Oh dear, oh dear.

NATHAN: Benet, you're a rabbit and getting married hasn't helped you much.

BENET: I felt so sorry about it. Ever since then I keep seeing the empty chair at your dinner where I was supposed to sit.

LAMAL: (Soothingly.) Yes, Nathan, we all worried about the embarrassment we caused you. Three empty places aren't nice to think about.

HAVER: That's right. I also apologize for that.

NATHAN: Oh, you needn't to have worried. I had no trouble filling your places.

HAVER: (Astonished.) You didn't?

LAMAL: You were able to find other important guests at such a late hour?

BENET: How lucky for you.

NATHAN: (Dryly.) Yes, wasn't it. As a matter of fact,

your replacements are here again tonight. Marcus, suppose you go and bring them out for a moment to meet my *former* friends. (NATHAN *whispers in* MARCUS' *ear.* MARCUS *laughs and exits.*)

LAMAL: *(Smoothly.)* You've taken a great load off our minds. Nathan. We all felt very badly about letting you down, even though circumstances prevented our being present with you that evening. We were talking about it on the way here tonight.

BENET: We were? I don't remember that.

LAMAL: *(Pulls him to one side.)* What next! Can't you agree with anything I say? Idiot!

HAVER: Imbecile!

LAMAL: Stupid oaf. Why did you insist on bringing him, Haver?

HAVER: Me? It was your idea.

LAMAL: Mine? I like that.

NATHAN: *(Laughing.)* Your love for each other is touching. (MARCUS *enters with* LYDA, KEM, *and* GARDIS.) But here's Marcus with my guests. Lamal, I would like you to meet Lyda who took your place at the feast. (LYDA *bows.*)

LAMAL: *(Shocked.)* This woman took my place?

NATHAN: Don't look so shocked. Lyda isn't a prominent citizen and landowner. She doesn't have property down by the lake. But she had the proper qualifications to attend my feast. She was willing to come and she was hungry.

LAMAL: This is an insult. Inviting her to take my place—my place at the head table!

NATHAN: Oh, she didn't mind sitting there. You see, Kem here sat beside her. *(Puts his arm around* KEM. KEM *and* LYDA *both laugh.)* Kem occupied your seat, Haver. And he did remarkably well, all things considered. Kem has no one to look after him so he steals when he gets hungry. But he hasn't had to steal since he's been my guest at dinner.

HAVER: *(Sputtering in anger.)* You—you put a thief in my place. You let this rascal sit at the head table as a distinguished guest? I've never heard of such actions in my life. You must be mad, Nathan.

NATHAN: I don't think so. I'm just learning who my real friends are.

BENET: *(Indicating* GARDIS) I suppose this old man sat where I was supposed to sit?

NATHAN: You're right, Benet. He has no new life to keep him home. In fact he has no one to care for him, no one except me. Marcus found him wandering around the garbage dump in the city, looking for something to eat. He's fared a great deal better in your place, Benet. Haven't you, Gardis? (GARDIS *bows and laughs.)*

BENET: I may be as stupid as Haver and Lamal say I am but I know when I've been insulted.

HAVER: That's the right word. We've been insulted publicly by you, Nathan.

LAMAL: *(Losing his cool.)* We certainly have. We came to apologize to you but now we find it's you who should apologize to us for such outrageous actions. An old woman, a thief, and a garbage scrounger. A fine lot to invite for dinner.

HAVER: That's right. I'm not against giving some scraps of food to the poor. It would have been all right to let these three eat the left-overs. But to treat them like equals, to put them in our places of honor—it's absolutely unbelievable.

NATHAN: *(Angry and disgusted. Facing the three men.)* No, it's you three who are unbelievable—staying away from my dinner yourselves, giving me flimsy excuses, and then objecting that others took your places. But I might have expected it from you three false friends. I was almost taken in by your apologies and your pious speeches but now I see you for what you are. You're selfish and completely self-centered. That's why you didn't come in the first place and why you want to creep back in now. Selfishness, that's the explanation for all three of you.

LAMAL: I, selfish?

HAVER: How can you say such a thing about me?

BENET: Am I really selfish? I thought I was only stupid.

NATHAN: You are all stupid. You thought you could use me to suit your own fancy, coming when it pleased you and staying away when you had something else you wanted to do. Well, if a man wants to be my friend, he can't let other things crowd out his love for me. I give my feasts for those who love me, not for those who love themselves.

HAVER: I still say you have insulted us by your actions.

NATHAN: Have I? Since when is it an insult to feed the hungry, to help the poor, to take care of the old and the infirm? These three, *(Indicating* LYDA, KEM, *and* GARDIS.*)* and the others at my dinner are my true friends. They come because I ask them. They eat because they enjoy my food. They are filled because I love them and they make me happy because *they* are happy. Come, my friends, back to the feast. *(They hurry away, laughing.)* And Marcus, shut the door. These three will not be allowed in my house. Ever. (NATHAN *exits.* MARCUS *takes the chair off and closes the door.)*

HAVER: Well, that was a failure. We've fixed ourselves with Nathan for good.

LAMAL: It's all Benet's fault. Why did you have to mention those empty chairs? That's what got us into trouble, after I had almost gotten things smoothed out.

BENET: We were in trouble when we said "no" to Nathan's invitation. *(To audience.)* I may be a fool but even *I* have sense enough to see that. *(Exit or Curtain.)*

Come Feast with Me

Text: Luke 14:15-24

The parable of the great feast finds response in the heart of every church worker. It all sounds so familiar and so exasperating. Invite a man to come to church with you and he will probably reply with an excuse. Ask someone to accept an office in the Sunday school and you will often get an excuse. Seek to raise money for a worthy cause and it is amazing how you always choose the wrong time for such an appeal.

No wonder our attention is almost automatically attracted to the sentence in the parable; "But they all alike began to make excuses." For we have heard and have probably given excuses ourselves. It is a common failing. And most excuses are so weak and so transparent that we wish people would not bother with them. Our response to this parable is, "Why didn't the men simply admit they didn't want to attend the banquet in the first place?"

Right there we have put our finger on the real

emphasis of the story. It's a story about a banquet, about a feast. It's not really about excuses, phony or otherwise. It's tempting to whale away at all who give excuses, but the important thing this parable teaches each of us is, "You have been invited to a feast." This is a happy parable for those who heed its message. Let's take a look at what is included in that simple theme, "You have been invited to a feast."

Suppose we begin with the last word—*feast* or *banquet*. A whole area of Christian truth is contained in that one word. It reminds us that ours is a religion of joy, of grace, of blessing. The kingdom of God is a land of rejoicing. Note how often Jesus talks about banquets, marriage suppers, full harvests, and other symbols of joy. The very name we apply to our basic message—gospel—speaks of good news.

Of course there's more to it than that. There are responsibilities as well as joys for the believer. There are times of sorrow and of persecution in the life of the church and of the individual. But Paul and Silas reflected the true spirit of believers when they sang in prison. They weren't incurable optimists and they weren't so stupid that they failed to realize they were in danger. They simply knew that they had been invited to a banquet when they had become believers and nothing could change that fact.

You and I need to catch that note too. Sometimes we get so bowed down by the worries and routines of daily existence, so discouraged by the temporary setbacks in our faith that we forget Christianity should bring us joy, not misery. David L. Edwards in his book, *The Last Things Now* says, "Reversing the emphasis in their Lord's own teaching, Chris-

tians think of their lives as battles not banquets."
Such an attitude is worse than heretical for it robs
each of us of the good news that "I am invited to
a feast."

Now let's take the sentence we have been using
as a theme and put the emphasis at the beginning:
"*You* have been invited to a feast." The word *you*
in the English language has a double meaning for
it can speak of one individual or many. And both
meanings are involved in this parable.

For Jesus is here speaking of the all-encompassing
nature of the gospel. That means that you and I
as individuals are welcome. But so is everyone else.
There is no elitism, no special privilege as far as the
gospel is concerned. We must not push the parable
so that it says that some get into the kingdom because others fail to show up, any more than we take
the phrase "compel them to come in" to mean that
men are to be made Christians against their will.

But the stress in the parable is not simply on all
being welcome. Those who come to the feast include
the poor, the maimed, the blind, the lame, indeed
people from the highways and hedges. Why this
rather peculiar concentration on the unimportant?
Why does Jesus so often stress that publicans and
sinners, thieves and harlots are welcome in his kingdom? Well, of course this emphasizes the all inclu-
siveness of the gospel call. If those usually regarded
as the dregs of society also are admitted to the kingdom, no one should feel he is excluded.

But there is something deeper behind this stress
on unimportant individuals. Jesus knew how we are
tempted to draw lines to exclude certain ones. He
knew the pride in the human heart. And so by word

and deed our Lord made plain that we neglect certain ones at our peril. No one is to be excluded. William Booth, the founder of the Salvation Army had the right attitude when he gave the command to his followers: "Go for souls and go for the worst."

This same attitude was expressed under different circumstances when the late King George V of England made a visit to a veterans' hospital to see all the war casualties there. When he got to one room he was told that the men inside were too scarred for the king to see. "I said all," he replied, "and I meant all." Our king also said *all* and he meant it. Jesus means that you must invite to his banquet the ugly-tempered foul-mouthed neighbor, the gossipy woman who irks you so, the teen-ager who annoys you with her transistor radio, and the old man who grumbles no matter how you try to help him. All are welcome. No one is excluded.

Suppose we take one last look at our theme and this time put the emphasis in the middle. You are *invited* to a feast. *Invited.* That word indicates that there is a choice to make. In Jesus' day a man received a preliminary announcement concerning a banquet and then a second invitation when all was ready. But he still could refuse if he chose to do so. And our relationship to our Lord is on this basis too. God operates by invitation, not only when we come into his kingdom but in all our actions toward him. No one can make you give; no one can make you serve. You have the same liberty the men in the parable had.

The church has often had arguments about this subject, about whether people are predestined to do this or that. Learned men have hurled ideas back and forth and they will probably continue to do so. But perhaps this simple parable contains the best answer for most of us. We have been invited. God invites all to serve him. But we can make excuses if we choose to do so.

And perhaps it is at this point that both the drama and this message can speak to us during the Advent season. For Advent tells us about the gracious coming of our Lord to this earth to bring men salvation. Advent involves invitation to the banquet God has prepared for all men. In this season we are told, "Here is new life. Here is goodness and joy for all." And you and I must respond to this invitation. Many of us, perhaps all of us have responded in the past, but each year at Advent we hear again the call of the Lord,—"Come feast with me." Let us today renew our faith. Let us say yes to God. No excuses this time. Let's come to the feast.

The Tower Builder and the King

Luke 14:27-33
SECOND SUNDAY IN ADVENT

DRAMA	**The Costly Life**
MEDITATION	**Everyday Martyrs**

The Costly Life

Based on Luke 14:27-33. The parable may be read before the play but this is not necessary.

CHARACTERS

JIM MILLER: business manager, brash, self-confident

MARJORIE BIDDEN: publicity writer, rather intense in her views

PASTOR SCHMIDT: a man of spiritual power but a bit discouraged

MRS. CARLISLE: middle-aged, devout Christian

MR. CARLISLE: harsh, loud, inconsiderate

SETTING

Sitting room in a hotel suite. Three chairs, table, and other furniture as desired.

COSTUMES

Usual contemporary costumes, JIM a bit loud, PASTOR SCHMIDT in a clerical garb if desired. Others, usual clothing.

(As the scene opens, JIM and MARJORIE come into the room and make themselves comfortable.)

JIM: Well, another sellout and a smash performance.

MARJORIE: Jim! Sounds like you're talking about a rock-and-roll singer or a football star instead of a pastor.

JIM: Maybe so. But right now Pastor Schmidt can outdraw any singer or athlete in the country.

MARJORIE: You're right. It's amazing the way people flock to hear him.

JIM: Nothing amazing about it. Where else can you find a man with a story like Pastor Schmidt's? Buried five years in a communist prison while the world thought he was dead. And then that escape with the help of two teen age girls. He stows away on a merchant ship and turns up in New York just in time to disrupt an international congress on peace and freedom.

MARJORIE: I know. The story's got everything—religion, suspense, intrigue, violence, sex—

JIM: And to top it all off, the man can speak like an angel. I've heard that talk of his a dozen times already and it still gets me right here *(pounds on heart)* each time I hear it.

MARJORIE: *(Laughing.)* The man must have something to get a hard old business manager like you right there *(pounds her heart)*.

JIM: Well, he does it every time. I think I could go on for the next ten years just booking Pastor Schmidt into churches so everyone could hear him.

MARJORIE: You'll have to count me out. I've only got six months leave from my magazine duties. That's my limit. But I have a feeling that this may prove a short assignment for both of us. Pastor Schmidt doesn't look good to me.

JIM: Nonsense. There's nothing wrong with him. Any man who can survive all he's been through has nothing to worry about. Besides, the doctors gave him a clean bill of health before we left New York and we've had him checked several times on this trip.

MARJORIE: I know that. He looks perfectly healthy, particularly when he's on that platform speaking to an audience. But something's wrong, Jim. Take a look at his face when he finishes his speech and sits down. I've done that the last two evenings and I don't like what I've seen.

JIM: (*Upset but trying not to show it.*) You're imagining things, Marjorie.

MARJORIE: Am I? Jim, he's got some kind of a struggle going on inside. And I don't think he's winning.

JIM: (*Agitated. Gets up and starts pacing the floor.*) Deliver me from women who think they're psychiatrists.

MARJORIE: (*Stung.*) Okay, okay. Keep up your masculine know-it-allness. But don't say I didn't warn you.

JIM: (*Still pacing.*) All right, I'll keep an eye on him. But I don't know what could be wrong. We put him up at good hotels like this one. He has everything he wants to make life pleasant. And the people flock around him by the thousands. *(An idea.)* Say, maybe that's the trouble. He doesn't have much time to himself, and people can be a nuisance, no matter how much you like them. But I'll watch that too from now on.

MARJORIE: Sh, I think I hear him coming. (PASTOR SCHMIDT *enters. He looks tired and worried.* JIM *and* MARJORIE *stand up.)*

JIM: Ah, Pastor Schmidt. Marjorie and I hurried ahead to make sure everything was okay here in the hotel.

SCHMIDT: *(He may speak with an accent but this isn't necessary.)* Very kind of you. Sorry to take so long coming from the church but there were so many who wanted to talk to me. It's been a long evening. *(Sinks into chair.)*

MARJORIE: *(Sitting down.)* I'm sure it has. The crowds were bigger tonight than at any time up to now.

SCHMIDT: Your news dispatches may have had something to do with that.

JIM: *(Still standing.)* Don't you believe it. You're the one who's making the impression. I don't mind telling you, Pastor Schmidt, I've managed a lot of speakers in my time but you're the best yet.

SCHMIDT: You're very kind, my friend.

JIM: Not a bit of it. Your message tonight was outstanding.

SCHMIDT: It's the same one I've been giving every-place.

JIM: I know. But you seemed to put even more spirit into it tonight.

SCHMIDT: Maybe it was—ah—desperation, not spirit.

MARJORIE: Desperation?

SCHMIDT: Yes. I think that's the English word I want. Tell me, Jim, how many more lectures am I supposed to give?

JIM: Well, let's see. (*Sits down and takes out schedule book.*) This is Memphis. Next comes New Orleans, then three speeches in Texas and on to the west coast. You get a little break there because we have a week at a retreat, then we really get going with a swing up and down the coast before we head back east—

SCHMIDT: Hmm. Jim, how long would it take to cancel those engagements?

JIM: Cancel them!

MARJORIE: Here it comes. I warned you.

JIM: But Pastor Schmidt—

SCHMIDT: Jim, I don't want to give any more speeches.

JIM: But this is crazy. You're the biggest drawing card in the country today. And we're just beginning. The biggest crowds are still ahead.

SCHMIDT: I'm sure I can continue to draw crowds for some time. But so can a two-headed calf, you know.

MARJORIE: Pastor Schmidt, you don't realize what your lectures mean to the church in America today. You're giving people new hope, you're making them think maybe Christianity hasn't lost its power after all. A two-headed calf can't do that.

JIM: *(Eagerly.)* And remember all that money you're collecting for poor people in Asia and Africa. You've done the best job of raising money for the church that's been done in years.

SCHMIDT: I'll be sorry to disappoint my friends and to fail the people who need money. But I have to do what my conscience tells me to. And everything inside of me says to stop this foolish lecturing.

JIM: But why, why?

SCHMIDT: It's a little hard to explain. Tell me, Jim, are you a Christian?

JIM: Sure. I wouldn't have taken this job if I hadn't been. You know I'm a Christian. That was one of the first things you asked me.

SCHMIDT: I know. I only wanted to hear you say it again. And you, Marjorie?

MARJORIE: You know my answer too. Of course I'm a Christian.

SCHMIDT: All right. Now let me ask you—What does it cost you to be a Christian?—Jim?

JIM: Cost? Well, I don't know. I do pay my church dues regularly, even though I'm not at home very much.

SCHMIDT: I see. It costs you a *tip* for God. And you, Marjorie?

MARJORIE: Well—I don't suppose it costs me very much. Being a Christian does keep me from doing some things that other people do.

SCHMIDT: Things that you shouldn't do anyway? (MARJORIE *nods.*) Some cost!

MARJORIE: I guess you're right.

SCHMIDT: I think I am. And there's my trouble. Christianity seems too easy, too painless for people here. Don't you see? I've spent five years in prison for my faith. Five years of my life, locked in a cell, forced to get up, to eat, to sleep, even to laugh or cry when my jailors ordered me to. And here it's all different.

MARJORIE: But even in your country, everybody didn't have to go to jail because he was a Christian.

SCHMIDT: I know. But there was always that possibility hanging over us. Choosing Christ still means risk for my people. It means being different, being looked down on, even being physically attacked. But here in your land it doesn't seem to mean anything at all. Christianity doesn't cost here. I know I can continue to draw crowds. And they all seem nice people. They come and they give money and they shake my hand when the service is over. And then they get into their comfortable cars and drive to their comfortable homes. The only cost for such people is that they've had to spend an evening away from their television sets. Am I wrong?

MARJORIE: *(After a pause.)* I can't say that you are.

JIM: I can't either. But at least your lectures make people think. Maybe it makes them see that Christianity does cost some people a great deal.

SCHMIDT: I'm afraid hearing me only makes your people feel more smug and self-satisfied with themselves. A man said to me tonight after my lecture, "We ought to bomb those heathen off the globe. All of them. Then the good Christian people could have some peace and quiet." But Christ didn't come to give people peace and quiet. He came to call us to service and sacrifice.

MARJORIE: You mustn't let one man's silly ideas upset you.

SCHMIDT: It's not just one man. This feeling of frustration has been coming on ever since I arrived here in America. Tonight I feel that I can't stand any more of this pretense.

JIM: But what will you do, Pastor Schmidt?

SCHMIDT: I want to go home.

MARJORIE: *(Shocked.)* Home! Why they'll put you in jail again. They might even execute you.

SCHMIDT: That's a real possibility.

JIM: Man, that's crazy.

SCHMIDT: Is it? Jesus didn't run away. He paid the full cost for his faith.

JIM: But you're not Jesus.

SCHMIDT: No, only a follower. But I've been a foolish follower, thinking peace and freedom were possible for me while others suffered. Well, I've been wrong. Every night I hear the prison doors slamming on the men and women I left behind. Every night I see the love and the terror in their faces. Who am I to sit in this comfortable hotel room while others are suffering and witnessing for Jesus? It's not right, not right for me. You've all been very kind but I want to go back and face my enemies. That's better than being smothered by your friends.

JIM: (*Carried away by the eloquence.*) Maybe you're right, Pastor Schmidt. I don't know. But give this a little time. Sleep on it at least. You're tired and we're all tired. Maybe things will look different in the morning.

SCHMIDT: Maybe so. But I doubt it. (*Knock at door.* SCHMIDT *moves to answer it but* JIM *motions him back into chair.*)

JIM: Let me answer it. I'll get rid of whoever is there. You need some rest. We all do. (JIM *goes to door and opens it.* MRS. CARLISLE *is heard but not seen until she enters.*)

MRS. CARLISLE: Please, may I see Pastor Schmidt? They told me at the desk downstairs that he was here.

JIM: He is here, ma'am. But he's too tired to see anyone tonight.

MRS. CARLISLE: It's important that I see him. Only for a moment—

JIM: Look, can't you come tomorrow morning? Or write him a letter?

MRS. CARLISLE: No, it's got to be tonight. Please—

JIM: I'm afraid—

SCHMIDT: Let her in, Jim. *(He gets up and* JIM *opens door all the way.* MRS. CARLISLE *enters.)* Come in, ma'am. I'm Pastor Schmidt.

MRS. CARLISLE: I know. I heard you speak tonight. I'm Mrs. Carlisle.

SCHMIDT: I see. This is Jim Miller, my business manager and Marjorie Bidden, my publicity—gal —I believe they call her.

JIM: Hello.

MARJORIE: How do you do.

MRS. CARLISLE: I'm pleased to meet you.

SCHMIDT: Won't you sit down?

MRS. CARLISLE: Just for a moment. *(She sits.* SCHMIDT *also sits,* JIM *and* MARJORIE *remain standing.)*

MARJORIE: Shall we leave?

MRS. CARLISLE: Please don't, on my account. (MAR-JORIE *sits.* JIM *remains standing as there are only three chairs.)* Pastor Schmidt, I felt I had to see you just for a moment to tell you what your message meant to me tonight. You've given me courage to go on being a Christian and somehow I felt I had to come and tell you.

SCHMIDT: It's very kind of you. But I don't understand what my story about being in prison could have said to you? What's been troubling you?

MRS. CARLISLE: Nothing that lots of others haven't had to face. You see, my husband isn't a Christian. He's a good man in many ways but he doesn't go to church and he doesn't want me to go either. He's always made things unpleasant about religion. Tonight he caused so much trouble that I decided that this was the last time I'd ever go to church. I'd just stay home and keep peace.

JIM: *(Sensing an opening.)* And when you heard Pastor Schmidt tell about *his* troubles, you decided you should be willing to take a little guff from your husband, eh? Is that it?

MRS. CARLISLE: *(Reluctantly.)* I guess so. That and his being here, taking time to tell us all about it.

MARJORIE: Mrs. Carlisle, this will make a great story for the magazine I work for. You're a Christian who's suffered, just like Pastor Schmidt has.

MRS. CARLISLE: Oh no. Nothing like that. But Pastor Schmidt, you made me see that I should be a Christian where God has placed me, regardless of the cost. That's what's given me help. And now I must be going.

SCHMIDT: You've been very kind. *(All standing.)* I thank you for coming. *(Loud knock at the door. MRS. CARLISLE seems to shrink back in anticipation of trouble.)*

JIM: I'll get it. *(Opens door.)*

CARLISLE: Is my wife here?

JIM: I don't know your wife.

CARLISLE: I know she's here. Get out of my way. *(Rushes in.)*

MRS. CARLISLE: Carl, I—

CARLISLE: Lily, I've been waiting outside the church for five minutes.

MRS. CARLISLE: I'm sorry, dear. I was coming right back.

CARLISLE: Lucky someone told me you were here. You're coming home right now. I'm missing part of a football game as it is.

MRS. CARLISLE: Let me introduce you to these people first.

CARLISLE: Don't want to meet them. I've met some of your church friends before. All sissies and fools. Come on.

MRS. CARLISLE: All right, dear. Goodbye, Pastor Schmidt. Don't worry about me. I'll not weaken again.

CARLISLE: Come on, Lily. *(He almost drags her out.)*

ALL: Goodbye, goodbye. (JIM *closes the door.*)

MARJORIE: *(Sitting down again.)* Whew, what a man.

JIM: It takes all kinds, but you wonder about some of them. I'm sorry, Pastor Schmidt, for all the noise and interruption.

SCHMIDT: Don't apologize. She was a messenger from heaven.

JIM: *(Eagerly.)* She did show you that you were wrong about a few things, didn't she?

SCHMIDT: That I should have been so proud as to think I was the only one suffering for my faith! Who can tell what lies behind the faces in an andience, what tears, what troubles. *(This speech almost as if to himself.)*

MARJORIE: I still think I can make this into a real human interest story for my magazine—changing the names and circumstances a bit of course. I wouldn't want to cause that good woman any embarrassment.

JIM: Pastor Schmidt, this experience tonight ought to convince you that you're needed here.

MARJORIE: Yes. Doesn't that make you feel you ought to stay?

SCHMIDT: I'm afraid not. It did make me see that there's a cost to the gospel—here as well as in my native land.

JIM: I see.

MARJORIE: I was hoping—

JIM: Well, that does it. I might as well begin cancelling those lecture engagements tonight. If Mrs. Carlisle didn't make you change your mind, nothing else is going to do it. *(Starts toward door.)*

SCHMIDT: Jim, come back here. (JIM *stops and turns back.*) I'm afraid you both missed what Mrs. Carlisle said that was *really* important.

MARJORIE: What was that?

SCHMIDT: She said she was going to be a Christian where God had placed her. And that was the real message from God to me.

JIM: I don't understand.

SCHMIDT: Jim, God allowed me to suffer in a communist prison for five years. That was the price I had to pay then. Then God allowed me to escape and suffer pursuit and terror until I came to this country. That too was a price. Now God has put me into this comfortable hotel, on a lecture tour, telling my story to others. That's the price of my faith now. I've been foolish enough to think that the cost is always the same, for everyone, all the time. That's not so. Prosperity and comfort may be a part of the cost too. Perhaps they are the highest a Christian has to pay as he seeks to serve his Lord.

MARJORIE: *(Eagerly.)* Then you're going to go on with the lecture tour?

SCHMIDT: Yes, until God opens another door for me. Jim, you may cancel your cancellations.

JIM: Thank God. And thanks to Mrs. Carlisle.

SCHMIDT: Amen. *(He shakes* JIM's *hand as curtain falls or scene ends.)*

Everyday Martyrs

Text: Luke 14:27-33

Words often become debased in meaning over the centuries. Thus to call a young girl "homely" was once considered a compliment. It indicated she was good, wholesome, worthwhile. But today, no young man in his right mind would tell his girl friend that she is homely and expect her to be pleased. The word has "come down" in meaning. Similarly the word "meek" has lost much of its original virtue. No one wants to be called "meek" today for this seems to imply that the individual has a milk-toast or doormat disposition.

The grand old word "martyr" has also suffered some loss. Once a martyr was a great hero of the faith. The word described a man or woman who was willing to endure punishment and even death rather than deny the Lord. "The blood of the martyrs is the seed of the church," men said and there was no prouder title than that of martyr. Today the word has sunk so that we use it to describe a self-pitying individual who "makes a martyr of himself," or we warn, "Don't be a martyr." Martyrdom is out of fashion.

And yet the word "martyr" has an important function in the vocabulary of Christianity for it reminds us that our faith costs, that being a follower of Jesus Christ is never an easy task. That's the warning implied in the parable of the tower and in the story of the king who starts out to fight a battle. "There is a cost," Jesus says, "consider it carefully." Note that the parables are preceded and followed by stern words of our Lord as he speaks of bearing the cross and of renouncing all that we have.

Such a warning was hardly necessary for the first band of Christians however. They saw their leaders being killed because of their faith. Christians were despised and slandered by their neighbors, even being called atheists and cannibals. From time to time terrible persecutions swept over the church and lengthened the roll of martyrs. For a minister in those days to stand up and say, "Remember, Christianity costs," would have invited the response; "So what else is new." The church realized and warned every convert that faith in Christ could mean suffering and death.

Today, however, the message of these two parables needs emphasis and reiteration. The word "martyr" has lost its punch. This has happened of course because the more violent forms of persecution have largely disappeared. Even where there is official opposition to Christianity the attacks are more muted and concealed. The great age of martyrs seems over.

But this need for emphasis on the cost of our faith has also arisen because we have done a "selling job" on Christianity. In our eagerness to get people into the church we have played down the idea of cost, of martyrdom. We have associated Christianity with peace of mind, good health, and material blessings and have stopped there. If you think this is a false picture, ask yourself how much warning you were given before you joined the church. Did anyone tell you that your faith might cost something beside the weekly offering?

This soft-sell technique is very dangerous for the believer. For when we have received no warning of trouble, we are more upset and disturbed when it does occur. It's like taking a wonder drug without being told that there are some side effects possible. This is why so many people get angry or disturbed and leave the church. They simply didn't expect unpleasantness or sacrifice or maryrdom as a part of their allegiance to Christ.

So let's say it loud and clear. If you haven't heard it before, hear it now. Christianity costs. It makes demands on you. *It hurts.* If you are going to serve Jesus Christ, count the cost. Paul puts it plainly by demanding that we present our bodies as living sacrifices. Dietrich Bonhoeffer said that when Christ calls a man, he calls him to die. And while that is seldom literally true, Christianity always involves surrender and the willingness to pay the cost, no matter what that may be.

But we seem to have gotten ourselves into a tangle. If we are called on to suffer martyrdom and yet martyrdom is only a remote possibility, that's like being all dressed up with no place to go. What's the use of saying that Christianity costs when most of us are called on to make only meagre sacrifices for the gospel. Should we go out and seek trouble in order to demonstrate that we are willing to bear the cross? Obviously not. Jesus told his own disciples that when they were persecuted in one town, they should flee to another. They were not to ask for trouble and neither are we.

What we must realize is that the cost of our faith is always something imposed from the outside. The reason one Christian dies as a martyr and another lives an undisturbed life is not because of individual choice but external circumstances. T. S. Eliot in his famous play, *Murder in the Cathedral* has Thomas Becket explain this very well. Says the soon to be martyred Becket: "A martyrdom is never the design of man; for the true martyr is he who has become the instrument of God, who has lost his will in the will of God, not lost it but found it, for he has found freedom in submission to God." In other words, the cost is the same for all of us. We are to live our lives in harmony with God and martyrdom then becomes a matter of indifference or chance for us.

Dwight Moody knew this lesson very well. Someone once asked him if he had enough faith to be burned at the stake. "No, sir," Mr. Moody replied honestly. When asked if he wished he did have, Moody simply said, "No. What I want is faith enough to help me get through a Sunday school teacher's convention scheduled for next week." Moody recognized that God wants us to take life as it comes, aware of the blessings and burdens of our faith but trusting that with God's help we can meet whatever cost is demanded. In short, this is what it means to be a martyr every day—to count the cost and yet face life unafraid.

Advent has that air about it. It is a time when we once again hear the call of our Lord to follow him. And perhaps it is a time to be reminded of those strange words of advice John the Baptist gave to those who came to him for help. He didn't tell anyone to go out and die for his faith. He simply indicated that each one should serve God in the place where God had put him. That's the cost for you and me today. If you heed the call of the Savior, that's what he asks of you.

The Rich Man and Lazarus

Luke 16:19-31
THIRD SUNDAY IN ADVENT

DRAMA	**What If . . . ?**
MEDITATION	**The Agony and the Ecstasy**

What If...?

Based on Luke 16:19-31. See reading instructions below.

CHARACTERS

ADAN: polite but sceptical; the oldest brother

OBED: a bit abrasive; a miracle monger

TOLAR: greedy, quarrelsome

MILICH: timid and a bit simple

ROSTAM: oily, smooth; a crook

LAZARUS: still a bit of a beggar; concerned

READER: may be played by man or woman

COSTUMES

May be played in biblical or modern costumes. The five brothers are well-dressed, with ROSTAM being the sharp looking one and TOLAR wearing the carefully patched clothes of a miser. LAZARUS should be dressed in rags.

SETTING

Simple stage setting. Four chairs are necessary, on stage right or left, opposite the entrance. Other furnishings can be added.

READER: *(Reads the parable and then adds:)* That's the way Jesus told the story of the rich man, often called Dives, and the beggar Lazarus. But suppose the story had been different. What if it went like this. *(Pretends to read from Bible.)* "Then I beg you, Father Abraham, to send Lazarus to my father's house for I have five brothers, so that he may warn them, lest they also come into this place of torment." And Abraham said, "That's a merciful proposal. Lazarus, I'm going to send you back to earth to meet with Dives' five brothers. Warn them of what lies ahead for them if they do not change their ways. Perhaps they can be saved and rescued for heaven." *(Looking up.)* Suppose that was the way the story went. What would have happened then?

*(*ADAN *is seated on one of the chairs.* OBED *enters and shakes hands with* ADAN *who refuses to get up.)*

OBED: Well, well, Adan. You're first, as usual. Father should have named you Adam.

ADAN: That's an old family joke, Obed. But I suppose I usually am first when the five of us meet. And Rostam will be last, if everyone runs true to form. How are you?

OBED: *(Sitting down.)* As good as can be expected at my age.

ADAN: Poof—at your age. You're younger than I am. Are they all coming?

OBED: Wild horses couldn't keep them away. Whoever wrote that letter composed a masterpiece, especially the phrase *(Reading from letter which he takes out of pocket or robe.)* "Will learn something of advantage to you."

ADAN: Sounds like lawyer talk to me.

OBED: Probably is. But it also has the smell of money about it. Oh they'll all be here, especially Tolar. He could smell out a shekel if you hid it in a block of cheese and buried it in the sea.

ADAN: *(Sarcastically.)* Most of our family have some *slight* interest in money, dear Obed.

OBED: I'll not argue that point. *(Turns and sees To-lar and Milich approaching.)* Ah, here come Tolar and Milich. *(They enter. Obed offers his hand.)* Good afternoon, dear brothers.

TOLAR: *(Turning away.)* Don't you dear brother me, Obed. I'm not speaking to you. *(Milich goes over and sits beside Adan, greeting him silently.)*

OBED: *(Lightly.)* What did I do now?

TOLAR: You bought that piece of property next to mine right out from under my nose.

OBED: You can cover a pretty good area with your nose, I'll agree. But you said you weren't interested.

TOLAR: That was just to beat the price down. You knew that. I don't intend to speak to you again today.

OBED: Well, that will be a relief. *(They glare at each other.)*

ADAN: *(In friendly tone.)* Maybe we'd better have a little chat while those two dogs growl at one another.

MILICH: *(Harshly.)* I'm not here to chat. Does anybody know what this is all about or are you all stupid as usual?

OBED: My, we're filled with brotherly love. All we need is Rostam with his oily tongue and the love feast can begin.

MILICH: Speak of the devil—. Here he comes now. (ROSTAM *enters.*)

ROSTAM: *(Feigned friendliness.)* Good afternoon, all. *(General replies and greetings.)* I hope everybody is in good health. Anyone show up yet to explain what this is all about? *(Waves letter.)*

ADAN: Not yet, Rostam.

ROSTAM: Hope we don't have to wait long. I have a lot of important matters to take care of today. *(Importantly.)* I'm busy, busy busy all the time.

TOLAR: Maybe you'd better go about your business then and leave us to take care of things here. We'll give you your share of money if there is any.

ROSTAM: *(Sarcastic.)* You'd like that, wouldn't you? And of course I can trust all of you, dear brothers. But I'm staying. Only I wish whoever called us together would show up.

OBED: *(Who has been watching the entrance.)* Someone is coming this way. *(They all stand and look.)* But it can't be the one we're expecting. It looks like a beggar.

ROSTAM: A beggar. He'll not get much from this crowd.

LAZARUS: *(As he enters, they shrink back from him and crowd into the other half of the room.)* Good afternoon, gentlemen. I see that you received my letter and are all present.

OBED: Your letter! Why you're a beggar, a ragpicker.

LAZARUS: That's right. I thought my usual earthly costume might make my story a little easier for you to understand.

ADAN: Why, I know you. You're the beggar Lazarus who used to lie outside the door at Dives' house.

LAZARUS: Correct, Adan, sir. (ADAN *is surprised at the use of his name.)*

ROSTAM: But that can't be. Lazarus died four months ago. I remember Dives mentioning it.

LAZARUS: That's right, Rostam, sir. I did die four months ago.

MILICH: *(Heading for door.)* Let me out of here.

OBED: *(Restraining him.)* Oh, for heaven's sake, shut up, Milich.

MILICH: I don't want to stay in a room with a beggar, whether he's dead or alive.

LAZARUS: Gentlemen, if you'll all sit down I'll try to explain everything and give you the important message I have for you.

TOLAR: That's a sensible suggestion. Besides, my feet are killing me.

ADAN: That's because you're always being carried around instead of walking.

OBED: *(Impatiently.)* Come on, let's stop quarrelling and hear what the man has to say. *(They head for the chairs and pull them to one side of the room. They are one chair short.)* I'll get you a chair, Milich.

MILICH: I would rather stand. As close to the door as possible. *(He edges toward the door.* LAZARUS *stands and faces the others.)*

LAZARUS: Thank you for your attention. As you have discovered, I am or I was Lazarus the beggar. I did die four months ago. And by the grace of God I was transferred to Abraham's bosom. Think of it—one minute I was lying in the dirt in front of Dives' door, the next minute I was in heaven. All my pain was gone, all my hunger satisfied, all my worries ended.

ROSTAM: I don't believe it.

LAZARUS: I assure you, it is true.

ROSTAM: What sort of a place must heaven be if beggars like you are admitted?

OBED: You don't need to worry about heaven, Rostam. Let the man get on with his story.

LAZARUS: Thank you. Two months ago, as you are all aware, your brother Dives died. I'm sorry to have to tell you that things did not turn out too well for him. One minute he was sitting in his beautiful home, the next he was in the flames of hell.

MILICH: What a shocking thing to say about Dives.

OBED: Come on, Milich. You didn't expect anything else, did you?

MILICH: No, but I don't like to be told about it.

LAZARUS: I don't like to have to tell you, either. But I'm here now at Dives' request. He feels responsible for all of you since he was the oldest brother. He begged and Abraham agreed that I should come and warn you to change your lives so you could escape the punishment that Dives is now suffering. That's why I'm here.

TOLAR: You didn't come to bring us any money or reveal where Dives buried some treasure?

LAZARUS: No. I came to warn you that your greediness will land all of you in torment if you don't change your ways.

MILICH: I've heard enough. I'm leaving right now.

LAZARUS: (*Trying to detain him.*) But Milich, sir, you mustn't go away like that. Your brother is concerned about you. He wants to save you from your foolish concern with money.

MILICH: I don't believe a word that you're saying. You're a demon, sent to deceive us.

LAZARUS: Why should I want to deceive you? If I'm a demon why should I warn you that you are in danger of losing your soul?

OBED: The man's right, Milich. Whatever he is, he certainly isn't a demon.

MILICH: *(Furious and frightened.)* Oh no? Look, people don't come back from the dead. But demons can take human shapes to deceive us.

OBED: How do you know that?

MILICH: Because nurse told us, years ago. You all remember how she used to scare us to death with her stories. But I never thought I would come face to face with a demon until today.

ADAN: What makes you think this man is a demon?

MILICH: He tells lies. He says he comes from Dives. But that can't be true. Dives never thought that much of any of us. He only thought about money and he taught me that money was the most important thing in the world. I believe it, and anybody who says it isn't must be a demon.

ADAN: That's logic for you.

MILICH: Shut up, Adan. I've got more money than you have. *(Whirls on Lazarus.)* And you—even if you are Lazarus, you were nothing but an old beggar on earth. What do you know about the value of anything? You're a demon, trying to steal my gold. Well, You'll not get away with it. The rest of you can stay here and fall under this sorcerer's power, but not me. I'm going home—and count my money. *(Exit.)*

LAZARUS: *(Calling.)* Milich. I'm sorry he felt like that. Dives will be very disappointed. Perhaps some of you other brothers can talk to Milich later.

ROSTAM: Don't worry about Milich. He always was

a little touched on the subject of demons. He's a fool. But I'm not. So what's your game, mister?

LAZARUS: *(Bewildered.)* My game?

ROSTAM: What are you up to?

LAZARUS: I've told you the purpose of my visit.

ROSTAM: Sure you have. And it's as smooth a story as I've ever heard. But what's the pay-off? What's it all going to cost us?

LAZARUS: There's no cost. Your money is of no value to me in heaven.

ROSTAM: Heaven! Do you think we're taken in by your story of being Lazarus, the beggar?

ADAN: He certainly looks like Lazarus.

ROSTAM: Don't be a fool, Adan. Who looks at a beggar's face? This fellow has simply dressed himself up like Lazarus and has fooled us with his fancy letter and his slick story. But why, why? What's the gimmick, beggar?

LAZARUS: I told you, I've come with a message from your brother in hell.

ROSTAM: My brother in hell. Now I get it. It's blackmail, isn't it?

TOLAR: Blackmail!

OBED: How do you figure that, Rostam?

ROSTAM: Very simple. Listen to that phrase, "your brother in hell." Not very nice, is it? Suppose this beggar goes around the neighborhood telling his yarn to everybody he meets.

LAZARUS: But I can't do that. I have to hurry back to heaven and make my report.

ROSTAM: Hurry back to heaven! The man's priceless. Can't you see what he's trying to do? He's going to demand that we pay him to keep quiet about all this. After all, it wouldn't be nice to have some of our friends ask us—how's your brother in hell today?

ADAN: I hadn't thought of that.

ROSTAM: No, but I'm sure he has. Now look here, Lazarus, or whatever your real name is. I'm not paying. You can get money out of the rest of them or you can blab your story to everybody in the community. I don't care. But you're not blackmailing me. That's my game to play on others.

LAZARUS: I see. You suspect me because that's what you would do?

ROSTAM: Maybe so. But I'm walking out. Get your money out of these other suckers if you can. You've got a good scheme, though. I admire a clever rascal. So long, brothers. *(Exit as they say goodbye.)*

LAZARUS: This is proving more difficult than I imagined. *(To the three remaining.)* I assure you that he's all wrong. I haven't asked you for a penny and I don't intend to do so. I'm only here to warn you that your love of money is going to land you in trouble.

ADAN: We all know Rostam. He's so crooked that he is sure everyone else is also a crook.

OBED: That's right. Now I'm impressed with you,

Lazarus, if that's your name. What you say may be true. But you can hardly expect us to believe all this, simply on your word. What proof can you give us that you're not a blackmailer or a demon or a madman?

LAZARUS: Doesn't the fact that I'm here vouch for my story? I *am* Lazarus, the beggar. Your eyes and ears tell you that. I did die. You all know that, too. What other proof do you need beside my presence here?

TOLAR: That all sounds logical, doesn't it, Obed?

OBED: Of course it *sounds* logical. But there are dozens of ways to explain what has happened. Maybe the beggar Lazarus wasn't really dead. People just thought he was. Maybe he had a twin brother. Maybe we've been hypnotized into accepting a clever impersonation. There are so many possibilities. I want more proof.

LAZARUS: What do you want me to do?

OBED: Anything. Make a chair float around the room. Turn Adan upside down and let him walk on the ceiling. Get a bottle of wine and change it into water. I only want to see a miracle or two and then I will believe you.

LAZARUS: I didn't come to perform miracles but to tell you the truth.

OBED: Not even one little miracle? One bit of hocus-pocus?

LAZARUS: You wouldn't be convinced even if I did any of the things you want done. You'd want another miracle tomorrow and still another the next day.

OBED: You know, I suspect you're right. You read me pretty well. Still, I'm not rejecting your story. I intend to keep an open mind about it.

LAZARUS: An open mind may let the truth fly through without stopping.

OBED: That's good. That's very good. I'll make a note about that and mull it over for a while.

LAZARUS: *(Exasperated.)* The fires of hell don't wait for mulling.

OBED: You're very smart, for a beggar. It would be a pleasure to sit down and discuss religion with you. But I think I must be going. I wish you could have done just one little miracle for me. Goodbye. *(Shakes hands.)* Perhaps I shall see you again.

LAZARUS: I'm sorry, but I doubt it. Goodbye, Obed. (OBED *exits.*) Well, we are down to two. Still, two's better than none.

ADAN: I'm sorry but you're down to one. I'm ready to leave.

LAZARUS: Not you too, Adan. I remember how you once gave me a shekel when you had put through a good business deal. I hoped to show you my gratitude with my message from Dives.

ADAN: Very clever, beggar. But I don't believe your story.

LAZARUS: Why not?

ADAN: For a very simple reason. I don't believe in heaven or hell. So I have no fear of any punishment when I die.

LAZARUS: But I've been in heaven. And seen hell.

ADAN: So you say. But that's all superstition to me. This world is heaven and it's also hell. What happens here is all there is. And this world is a hell if you don't have money. That's my philosophy. So I'm not taken in by any threats or promises for the future.

LAZARUS: Have you considered the consequences if you are wrong?

ADAN: *(Becoming agitated.)* I can't be wrong. I dare not be wrong. I've staked my whole life on that belief.

LAZARUS: I tell you, you *are* wrong. Life goes on and things get evened up in eternity. Think what it has meant to your brother Dives. Splendor and feasting here for a little while and then endless separation from God.

ADAN: No, no I tell you. When a man's dead, he's dead. That's the way I want it and that's the way it is.

LAZARUS: Don't be a fool, Adan. There's still time to change your life.

ADAN: Why did you come here to trouble me? You plant doubt in my mind where there was certainty. I won't listen to any more of this. I won't, I won't. *(Puts hands over ears and runs from room.)*

LAZARUS: *(Sadly.)* Well, Tolar, you're the only one left.

TOLAR: It looks that way.

LAZARUS: I thought you would be the hardest to convince. You do know that I'm Lazarus, don't you? Come back from the dead?

TOLAR: Yes. I don't have any doubts about that.

LAZARUS: And you know that I've come to bring you a message from your brother Dives?

TOLAR: Yes. I don't know whether he's moved by kindness or whether he simply doesn't want us in hell to accuse him of misleading us, but I believe your message comes from him.

LAZARUS: Thank God. My visit hasn't been in vain.

TOLAR: Don't get your hopes up, Lazarus. I'm not going to change, any more than the others.

LAZARUS: But why, why?

TOLAR: It's very simple. The money. *That* stands in the way.

LAZARUS: But the money won't do you any good when you're dead.

TOLAR: You're not asking me to give it up when I'm dead. You're asking me to change now.

LAZARUS: Tolar, I promise you. You'll have more joy right now if you give your money away than you ever had in piling it up. Believe me.

TOLAR: I'm not doubting anything you say. But I can't give it up.

LAZARUS: You must. It's become a god for you.

TOLAR: That's right. A god, a demon, a fever in the blood. The first thing I do every morning is count my money. The whole purpose of my life each day is to increase my wealth. The last thing I do every night is to make sure my money's safe. It's my life, my love, my whole existence.

LAZARUS: But you can change all that.

TOLAR: No, Lazarus. Because a man can't change unless he wants to. And I don't want to. Maybe there was a time when my life could have taken a different path. But I chose the road paved with gold and it's too late to turn back now.

LAZARUS: Don't say that.

TOLAR: I must. *(Extends hand.)* Thank you for coming, Lazarus. Even thank my brother Dives if you see him. *(Leaving, the old* TOLAR.*)* And tell him I've got more money now than he had when he died. Goodbye. *(Hurries from room.)*

LAZARUS: I've failed, I've failed. Father Abraham, they wouldn't listen. I couldn't move their gold-encrusted hearts.

READER: If they do not hear Moses and the prophets, neither will they be convinced if someone should rise from the dead.

The Agony and the Ecstasy

Text: Luke 16:19-31

Why doesn't everybody believe in Jesus Christ? If Christianity is true, why is it so hard to convince people that they should believe the gospel? There can be no complete answer to this question, of course. There is a mystery behind faith and doubt, a mystery that involves both God and man. Yet it is possible to list some things that cause people to refuse the gospel. And although this may seem a negative approach, it can lead us to a better understanding of our faith

Let's begin by admitting that some people have a closed mind on the subject. They refuse to listen, they refuse to consider the claims of Jesus Christ. Jesus frequently found that attitude displayed when he was here on earth and we are told that at one time he marvelled at the unbelief of his opponents. One of the striking examples of human pig-headedness took place when Peter and John healed the man at the Gate Beautiful. His opponents didn't deny that a remarkable healing had taken place; they simply took steps to prevent this type of thing happening again.

We should not be surprised at such an attitude however. Human prejudice is deep-rooted in many areas and people can be hard-headed or bull-headed about religion too. A good example of how men's minds work was provided when one of our moon rockets sent back pictures showing the earth floating in space like a ball. The president of the Flat-Earth Society when shown these pictures acknowledged that "to the uninformed" it looked as if the earth was round. But he refused to change his viewpoint. His mind was closed. Human beings can be equally stubborn about religion. Jesus said that he stands at the door and knocks, but if men have locked the door and thrown away the key, nothing can happen.

We must also recognize that God can get crowded out of the human heart by other things deemed more important. Jesus made it plain that a man can't serve two masters but many are only willing to give God second or third place at best and God will not accept that. The rich man in the parable evidently put money and pleasure before God, and so presumably did his five brothers. The rich young ruler fell into the same trap. Money, ambition, love of self, and a thousand and one other things can get in the way of God's truth.

When Jesus was here he was also bothered by people who wanted miracles and additional proof before they would believe. Even one of the disciples, Thomas, demanded tangible proof of the resurrection before he would accept Jesus' claims. And Thomas has countless followers in the world today. They want scientific proof of all the words of the Bible. They would like to put God in a test tube and analyze him before they will believe. They are not satisfied with "Moses and the prophets."

Why should we bother with this negative approach? Why list reasons for *not* believing the gospel? Well, to begin with, such views are a warning to every Christian. We dare not look smugly at the world, feeling very confident of our own superiority. For the believer is always in danger of making the same mistakes that others make. We can set up barriers between ourselves and God. We are not proof against hard-headedness or double-mindedness or miracle mongering. We too are called on to rely on the Word of God, on "Moses and the prophets." We will not receive any other revelation or help.

But perhaps more importantly, an understanding of unbelief helps to relieve some of the agony of Christian work. Somehow we have gotten the notion that the church should always continue to grow, that the gospel, which seems so true to us, should be eagerly accepted by others. And then comes the cold water of reality. Winning people for Christ isn't as easy as it sounds. Indeed we are all tempted to echo the words of Isaiah: "Who has believed our report?" Ministers and evangelism committees and every Christian who takes his responsibilities seriously have to face this agony at times.

Our first instinct is to feel that something is wrong with the church or the gospel. The church is old-fashioned and the message isn't being presented correctly. Now it is a good thing to be humble and to examine ourselves for faults. Undoubtedly Christians have often put stumbling blocks in the way of their

brothers in the world. But we do need to remember
the lesson of this parable. The fault may lie with the
person who is being approached. Jesus could not win
everyone for his kingdom. Even one of the disciples
turned traitor. Paul could not win everyone to whom
he witnessed. And we must face the fact that some
won't believe, no matter what we do. This is the
agony of church work but we must face it honestly
and recognize the simple truth: You can't win everyone for the gospel.

But let's not overlook the ecstasy. The beggar Lazarus is in Abraham's bosom. He has been moved from
a lifetime of misery to an eternity of joy. He seems,
at first glance, an extremely unlikely candidate for
heaven. Earthly life treated him harshly, a harshness
made more unbearable by the contrast with Dives,
the rich man. We might be inclined to sympathize
with Lazarus if he had been moved to denounce God
because of the unfairness of life. But the beggar believed and was saved.

And that's the joy of the gospel. We may not be
able to win all but we can win some. Thank God
that some believe. Thank God that we have as many
in the church as we do. Jesus spoke about joy in heaven when a sinner repents. There should be joy in
the church, indeed real ecstasy when a new member
is added to God's kingdom. Baptism should be a joy-
ful occasion and adult professions of faith should call
for shouts of "Praise the Lord." The believer should
never despair at the gospel for it still has power to
move men.

Agony and Ecstasy. All church work has that two-
fold characteristic. We feel it strongly in the Advent
season when the call to repentance goes out again as

it did in the days of John the Baptist and Jesus. We must face the unpleasant truth that some will not hear. They will be immersed in materialistic preparations for Christmas or other worldly pursuits. But thank God, some will hear and will come, seeking the Lord.

The Alert Servants and the Burglar

Luke 12:35-40
FOURTH SUNDAY IN ADVENT

DRAMA | **Easy Does It**

MEDITATION | **Now and Not Yet**

Easy Does It

Based on Luke 12:35-40. It will help the play if this brief parable is read before the singer begins the opening song although this is not absolutely necessary.

CHARACTERS

SINGER: a guitarist if desired; several singers may be used

MARG: rather sloppy but likeable woman

LILLIAN: carefully groomed, well organized

JAMES: egotistical, cock-sure business man

CARL: quieter, not a pusher

GRANDPA: old man, a putterer

SONNY: young boy, no older than 12 if possible

MR. ADAMS: middle-aged church leader

MRS. ADAMS: sincere, kindly

PETER: young man in early twenties or late teens

(Note: It is possible to cut one scene in the play or to double some of the characters but the parts are short and numbers help the impact of the play.)

SETTING

Setting is indicated for each scene. Props should be kept to a minimum.

COSTUMES

Contemporary.

(Play opens with the reading of the parable. Then SINGER sings the first verse of the song in a lazy, languid manner. Setting for first scene can be put in place as song is sung or be ready before the play opens.)

Take it eas-y, nice and slow. No use rush-ing to and fro. Too much hust-ling strength will tax. Eas-y does it, just re-lax.

(As scene opens, MARG is seated in a chair, drinking coffee. There is general disorder with things piled on chairs and floor. There is a knock at door.)

MARG: *(Calling.)* Come on in. (LILLIAN *enters.*) Oh, it's you, Lillian. Good to see you. *(Takes things off chair and piles on floor.)* Sit down and have a cup of coffee.

LILLIAN: *(Sits down.)* No thanks. Just had one a few minutes ago. Say, you look relaxed.

MARG: Oh, I am, I am. But I really shouldn't be.

LILLIAN: Why not?

MARG: Well, I'm expecting company a little later. Some business friends of Bill's are stopping by for a little while. Bill told me to be sure and make a good impression on them when they come.

Lillian: Well, this place will make an impression all right. I'm not sure how good it will be.

Marg: (*Good-naturedly.*) All right. No need to be sarcastic. I know it's a mess but we were up late last night and I just didn't get started very early today. In fact I'm not really started yet. But I'll get there.

Lillian: Well, I came by to see if you wanted to go down town and do some shopping. Guess I've got my answer to that. Maybe I'd better stay and help you clean up before your guests arrive.

Marg: Say, that would be nice. But no hurry. They won't be here for a while.

Lillian: What time are you expecting them?

Marg: I'm not sure. But they're coming over from Darlington and that should take a couple of hours. And they'll hardly start before nine o'clock. So I figure I've got plenty of time to straighten up before they arrive. You know I can really clean up in a hurry when I get started.

Lillian: I know. You're a regular white tornado when you do get under way. But you amaze me. How can you be so relaxed and so—unprepared?

Marg: It's no trouble. I just tell myself "easy does it," and take my time. I'll admit that occasionally I get caught. But not today, with you to help.

Lillian: Well, let's get at it. (*Gets up.*)

Marg: Not just yet, Lillian. I still have a little coffee to drink. And you didn't tell me what you were going down town for.

LILLIAN: Oh, I had a bit of shopping to do. Harry's birthday is coming up in a few weeks and I figure I might as well do some checking on things right now. I want to get him some new golf clubs. At a cheap price.

MARG: *(Surprised.)* You're going to buy them yourself?

LILLIAN: Sure, why not? I always pick out his birthday present.

MARG: You really are something. I generally wait until the last minute, get a card for Bill and tell him to get his own present.

LILLIAN: That's not very personal.

MARG: I know. One of these days I'm going to start out ahead of time and get him something real nice. At least I keep telling myself that. But I don't suppose I'll ever do it.

LILLIAN: Say, that sounded like a car door slamming out front. You don't suppose—

MARG: *(Complacently.)* Oh no.

LILLIAN: Sounds like some voices outside. *(Goes to window.)* Marg, some people are coming up the walk toward the house.

MARG: Here, let me get at that window. *(In terror.)* Lillian, it's them. I know it is. Here, help me pick up things. Quick, quick. *(They begin to run frantically to and fro, only making things worse.)*

LILLIAN: We'll never make it, Marg.

MARG: *(As knock sounds on door.)* No, we'll never make it. Never in a million years.

(Scene closes with blackout or curtain. The SINGER sings from the side of the stage. MARG and LILLIAN may join him if desired. The melody is the same but the tempo is speeded up and may be syncopated if desired.)

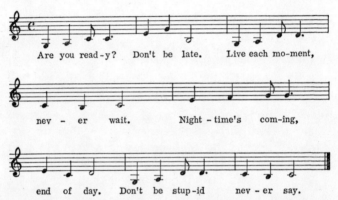

Are you read-y? Don't be late. Live each mo-ment,

nev - er wait. Night - time's com-ing,

end of day. Don't be stup-id nev - er say.

(Repeat the first verse in the languid tempo as before. During the singing, stage is readied for second scene, which requires two chairs and perhaps a small table. Men are seated and go into scene as singing ceases.)

CARL: Say, Jimmy, have you bought that new house yet?

JAMES: Well, practically.

CARL: What do you mean, practically?

JAMES: I'm going to buy it. I told you that. But the fellow still wants too much for it.

CARL: More than you're willing to pay, eh?

JAMES: Not really. But I figure he's asking about $500 more than he should. At least $500 more than he's willing to take. So I made him a bid of $1000 less than his asking figure. In another day or two he'll come down $500 and I'll go up $500 and I'll get the house at the price I wanted to pay in the first place.

CARL: Pretty shrewd business.

JAMES: Well, I've come to believe that the smart business man in this world is the one who can out-wait the other one. The fellow who doesn't act until the right moment picks up the marbles.

CARL: Sounds good. But aren't you afraid you might get fooled with all this waiting? Somebody else might step in and buy the place right under your nose.

JAMES: Not a chance. This fellow knows I want the house and nobody else will meet the price he's asking. Don't worry, I know what I'm doing. Jane and I have even decided where we're going to put the furniture. That's how sure I am that we're going to get that place. Say, how about you? You were looking for a house too.

CARL: Yes, but I never seem to find the right place.

JAMES: How about buying mine. I'll make you a good deal.

CARL: No thank you. It's too big and too expensive for my purse. Maybe I'll take a quick glance through the real estate ads before the boss gets here and insists that I do a little work today. (*Opens newspaper.*)

JAMES: Hope you find something good. The way Jane and I have.

CARL: *(Looking up from paper.)* Say, haven't you been dealing with Jones Realty Co.?

JAMES: Yeah. They have exclusive control over that property. Why?

CARL: Well, here's their ad. There's a picture of the property you've been looking at. But it's marked: "Sold."

JAMES: *(Snatches at paper.)* Here. Let me see that. *(Scans ad.)* Of all the nerve. They *have* sold it to someone else.

CARL: Guess they found someone to meet the guy's price.

JAMES: But I would have met it too, if I had thought—

CARL: Tough luck, Jimmy.

JAMES: Yes, tough luck.

CARL: If it was luck.

(Same business as before. The SINGER sings the second verse with the fast beat, followed by the slow first verse. CARL and JAMES may join the group. Scene is changed during singing. New scene requires only two old chairs, some pieces of metal and a cane. Tools can be added. As scene opens, GRANDPA is puttering and SONNY is just getting in the way.)

SONNY: Say, grandpa, what're you making?

GRANDPA: Oh, just an invention I've been tinkering with.

SONNY: What's it gonna be when you get it done?

GRANDPA: It's a combination cane and weed digger. I'm trying to fit this piece of iron onto the bottom of the cane. Then I'm going to put a spring inside and when you push a button in the handle, the weed digger will flip up and you'll have a cane to help you walk.

SONNY: Say, that sounds neat. You think you'll sell a lot of them when you get it all worked out?

GRANDPA: Nope. Only person who'd buy one would be a lame old man who wanted to dig weeds. And there aren't very many of them around.

SONNY: But how's come you're working on it if nobody will buy it?

GRANDPA: You ask too many questions, boy. I just like to tinker and think about what might have been.

SONNY: When I grow up I'm going to be an inventor too. I'll bet I'll invent something that'll sell a million, no, a zillion.

GRANDPA: Hope so, sonny. Only don't be a fool— like your grandpa.

SONNY: You're not a fool.

GRANDPA: Oh yes I am, or I was. Sit still for a few minutes and I'll tell you about it.

SONNY: *(Sits on chair.)* All right. But I've got to go play pretty soon.

GRANDPA: Play can wait. You remember what I tell

you because it's important. Sonny, you know I like to tinker and invent things.

SONNY: Oh yes, I know.

GRANDPA: Well, a long time ago I really invented something useful and valuable.

SONNY: *(Excited.)* You did! Did you make a lot of money?

GRANDPA: Not a penny. And that's because I was a fool. You see, I hit on a way of making radios cheaper and better. I invented a thing called a transistor.

SONNY: Oh, I've heard of them. You invented them, grandpa?

GRANDPA: I sure did. Made them and built them into a radio. Still got the model up in the attic.

SONNY: *(Enthusiastic.)* Can I see it? Can I?

GRANDPA: Sure. One of these days I'll take you up there and show you what a fool your grandpa was.

SONNY: But if you invented it, how could you be a fool? You have to be smart to make a radio.

GRANDPA: Oh, I was smart enough when it came to *making* it. So smart that I had to show it off to half the country. Then I took some time off to go on a little trip with your grandma. She'd been fussing at me for spending so much time with my invention. When I got back, I took my radio to a lawyer in the city to get what they call a patent so I could make radios like that one and nobody else could do it.

SONNY: Did you get your patent, grandpa?

GRANDPA: I got nothing. Just the week before, another fellow had gotten a patent for the same invention.

SONNY: *(Jumping up and down.)* He stole your invention. He stole it.

GRANDPA: No, he didn't. He had just been working along the same lines. I'd have beaten him if I hadn't fooled around. Never dreamed someone else might have the same idea. Thought I had plenty of time.

SONNY: Gee, that's too bad. Didn't you ever invent anything else that was any good?

GRANDPA: I'm afraid not, sonny. Learned my lesson too late. Well, you almost turned out to be the grandson of a millionaire, instead of a might-have-been. *(Stands up and walks away.)*

SONNY: *(Hugging him.)* I love you anyway, grandpa. But I wish you had been first.

GRANDPA: So do I, sonny, so do I.

(Same business as before. The SINGER *sings the second verse in a bouncy manner, followed by the languid first verse.* GRANDPA *and* SONNY *may join the group of singers. The scene is changed to a simple living room with three chairs. As the scene begins,*

MR. *and* MRS. ADAMS *are seated, talking to* PETER.*)*

MR. ADAMS: Peter, we're here from Christ Church to talk to you about a rather important matter.

PETER: *(Lightly.)* I see. What are you collecting money for this time?

MRS. ADAMS: We're not here to ask for money, Peter. What would make you think that?

PETER: Well, the only time anyone visits me from the church, he's after money. So I supposed this visit was like all the rest.

MR. ADAMS: I'm afraid we deserved that rebuke, Peter. But tonight we're after something more important than money.

PETER: *(Knowingly.)* What *could* you have in mind?

MR. ADAMS: You, Peter.

PETER: I was afraid that was it.

MRS. ADAMS: Look, Peter, We're not strangers to one another. I was a good friend of your mother's when she was alive. And she was a faithful member of the church all her life.

PETER: I know. She always made me go to Sunday school and church. Guess I've drifted away since she's been gone.

MR. ADAMS: We know. And we want you back, Peter. You were brought up as a Christian and we don't like to see you get away from the church.

PETER: I really haven't gotten away. I've just been taking a little vacation. I've been enjoying myself, been letting up on the religious bit for a while.

MR. ADAMS: But you can't turn your faith on and off like an electric light.

PETER: Why not? Lots of people do. I see people going to church now that didn't go a couple of years ago. You're not telling me that if I stay away for a while, I won't be allowed back in the church, are you?

MRS. ADAMS: Of course not, Peter. But it's dangerous business, gambling with your soul like that.

PETER: *(Getting up and walking around.)* Ah, now it comes. You're going to scare me now. You're going to say that I might die before I get back to my faith.

MRS. ADAMS: Death's always a possibility, Peter.

PETER: I know. Maybe you're even going to tell me that Jesus might return and I'd be left out—like the foolish virgins in the parable. You see, I know the technique.

MR. ADAMS: You're the one talking, not us, Peter.

PETER: But that's what you're thinking. Look, I'll come back to church one of these days if you'll leave me alone. But it's got to be my decision— when I'm ready.

MRS. ADAMS: Peter, no one wants to scare you or force you into anything you don't want to do.

PETER: *(Turning his back on them.)* Then leave me alone until I'm ready.

MRS. ADAMS: *(Hurt.)* All right, Peter.

PETER: I'm sorry if I sound rude but I don't want to be pushed.

MRS. ADAMS: As long as you're happy in what you're doing, Peter, we don't want to interfere. *(Standing up.)* Only, we do want you to know that we care about you. Mildred, I guess we'd better be going.

MRS. ADAMS: Yes, dear. Peter, we'll remember to pray for you. At least you can't keep us from doing that. (PETER *is in deep thought.*)

MR. ADAMS: *(Extending hand.)* Goodnight, Peter. (PETER *doesn't see it at first. Then he shakes hands.*)

PETER: Good night, Mr. and Mrs Adams. *(They start to leave.)* Wait a minute. Please.

MRS. ADAMS: What is it, Peter?

PETER: Mr. Adams, you said, as long as I'm happy. But I'm not.

MR. ADAMS: No, Peter.

PETER: How can I be, knowing that each day I've said "no" to the Lord again? How can I be happy, knowing I'm cheating God out of the good days of my life, saving for him what's left at the end if there is anything left at the end? That's what you've been trying to say to me, isn't it?

MR. ADAMS: You're saying it better than we can, Peter.

PETER: Is there still time for me? Still time to make things right?

MRS. ADAMS: Of course there's time.

MR. ADAMS: Yes, Peter. And the time is now.

(The SINGER *and the others join in the third verse
of the song.* PETER, MR. ADAMS, *and* MRS. ADAMS
*may join the group. The song is sung with joy and
exultation.)*

Are you read-y   for the Lord?   Are you trust-ing

in   his   word?   He   is   com-ing,

glor - ious day.   Love him, broth-er,   watch and pray.

*(Repeat the verse, this time changing the next to last
line to the words,* Love him, sister.*)*

Now and Not Yet

Text: Luke 12:35-40

Almost the last words of the Bible talk about a future event—the return of our Lord Jesus. Revelation 22:20 reads: "He who testifies these things says, 'Surely I am coming soon.' Amen, come Lord Jesus." Those words must have brought great joy to the readers of the book of Revelation. The church was undergoing persecution at that time and the promise of the second coming must have thrilled the early believers.

But almost nineteen hundred years have passed and our Lord has not returned. Christians still believe in the second coming; the doctrine is so interwoven in the New Testament that we can't tear it out. "The Son of man is coming at an hour which you do not expect," says our text and a similar statement appears in almost every New Testament book. But what can this truth say to us today? Isn't the second coming a dead doctrine, a teaching to be put in the dead letter file?

Not at all. The fact that the second coming seems delayed doesn't change its importance for us. For the promise of Jesus' return carries with it a strong emphasis on the *now*, on action now, on preparation now. The fact that the Lord delays his coming can never be used to say that we can delay too. For God is the God of eternity but we are men and women of the *now*.

Our text includes two parables but the emphasis is the same. In the first, a man has gone away and the servants are told to be ready for his return. In the second a householder is warned that the burglar will not announce his visit. In each parable the message is the same—watch. Be ready. Seize hold of the now.

I suspect that most of us need this stress. Procrastination, postponing is an almost universal human weakness, especially when it comes to religious matters. We love to salve our consciences with what we intend to do. The number of good actions that we have in mind is almost infinite. In the meanwhile, easy does it, no need to hurry. And to all this God's word says, *Now*. Do it now. Act and watch while it is time.

This is not to say that we are to be frightened by the second coming. Sometimes Jesus' words have been used in this fashion: "Hurry up or it will be too late." Don't sin because Jesus might return and catch you in the act. A small boy who went fishing one Sunday instead of going to church was told: "Suppose Jesus had returned today. What would you have said to him?" That's using the second coming as a club and God never seeks to make us behave by using a club. He simply wants us to use the present wisely

Benjamin Franklin used to draw up a list of goals at the start of each year and then seek to fulfill each goal during the year. There is some merit in Franklin's technique. I wonder what would happen if each one of us would write on a piece of paper today one good thing that we have intended to do for some time, and then would do it in the coming week. I imagine we would all be amazed at the amount of good that would occur in one week. But that's precisely the message involved in the second coming. Do it now. Accept God now. Serve and give now. Don't take it easy. Take heed and act now.

But the doctrine of the second coming has another meaning for us. Whether Jesus comes today or a thousand years from today, his promise to return reminds us that there is something ahead for Christians. What we have now is not what God intends for us. God has sent us Jesus Christ. And Christ has redeemed us and established the church where Christians can be in fellowship together. But that isn't all. Something still remains. God has another event on his calendar.

That truth is very important for us. For human beings can't live without hope. The word "hopelessness" is one of the most dismal in our language. A Christian dare never relapse into a state of hopelessness. Perhaps a parallel occurs in what happens to some people when they get old. They decide that life is over for them, that there is nothing to look forward to. So they simply exist in the past, in memories of happier days long ago. When that happens, death has come even though the individual may continue to exist for years.

We as believers are not to get into this frame of mind. We must not think that all the important things happened back in Bible times. The believer not only lives in the now but in the not yet. God still has something in store for us. Our text must not be interpreted to mean that we stand fast, contented to guard what we have. The return of our Lord will not only be unexpected but it will bring a wonderful change in human existence.

There are times when this doctrine has more meaning than at others of course. In days of persecution the church has always looked forward eagerly to the new life ahead. When men feel depressed, the promise of change is always welcome. In his book, *A Writer's Notebook* Somerset Maugham says "For no sensible person can deny that throughout the history of the world the sum of unhappiness has been far, far greater than the sum of happiness. Only in brief periods has man lived save in continual fear and danger of violent death, and it is not only in the savage state that his life has been solitary, poor, nasty, brutish and short." When our thinking runs along that line, what a comfort it is to remember that life doesn't stay frozen in that dreary pattern. There are good times ahead. In the "not yet" of the Bible there is hope for us in the future.

That's why in the Advent season we not only celebrate the first coming of Christ but also his second. For just as the first brought joy to human beings, the second will bring even greater joy. There is something ahead for all of us. We must be ready. We must live in the now and the not yet.

The Lost Sheep

Luke 15:4-7
CHRISTMAS

DRAMA	**The Lost Child**
MEDITATION	**Incredible but True**

The Lost Child

Based on Luke 15:4-7. The parable may be read before the play but this is not necessary.

CHARACTERS

NORMAN WILSON: young scientist, articulate, a bit cold at first

ELAINE WILSON: Norman's wife, not stuffy but sincere

MRS. PERRY: a bit older than the other two characters

BUZZ WILSON: about four or five, as young as possible

SETTING

Middle-class home, the living room with as much furniture as is desired. Only a few chairs are really necessary. And a phone.

COSTUMES

Contemporary. Not too elaborate since action takes place in the morning.

(NORMAN *enters. The room is empty. He calls.*)

NORMAN: Elaine. Buzz. I'm home.

ELAINE: *(Enters.)* Oh Norman, I'm glad. *(He kisses her lightly.)* You look tired, dear. Did you have any breakfast?

NORMAN: Yes, Les brought me some when he came to work.

ELAINE: It's been a long hard night for you, I know.

NORMAN: No, it hasn't. It's been peaceful and pleasant.

ELAINE: But this is the night you're all alone at the observatory.

NORMAN: I know. That's what made it so peaceful. Nobody around to disturb me.

ELAINE: I thought you liked the men you work with.

NORMAN: I do. They're a good gang. But when I'm looking through the big telescope, peering at some star that's millions of light years away, I like to be alone. I don't want to hear somebody moaning about last week's football scores or discussing which car gives the best gas mileage. Such stuff seems so petty, so unimportant compared to the stars around us.

ELAINE: *(Laughing.)* Norman, Norman. One of these days you'll get sucked up into that telescope and disappear into space.

NORMAN: *(Amused.)* Not likely. But there are times

when I wish I had trained to be an astronaut so I could *travel* in space, not just look at it.

ELAINE: Thank goodness you didn't do that. At least you get home a few hours each day now. Did you do anything special last night? Like, maybe discovering a new comet that you could name Elaine in my honor?

NORMAN: No such luck. Besides, the only things they give female names to are hurricanes.

ELAINE: You don't need to remind me of that. I think *Elaine* is on the list this year. Nothing exciting at the observatory then?

NORMAN: No, just routine. Spent some time checking on a Nova we've just spotted. Then had to assemble pictures of Jupiter, Venus, and Saturn for Doc Hennesy.

ELAINE: What's that for?

NORMAN: Oh, our annual Christmas madness. You see, some people claim the so-called star of Bethlehem was a conjunction, a lineup of those three planets and such a thing did occur in 7 B.C. So about this time of the year we always get a display together for visitors to the observatory. Then we have to answer umteen silly questions about whether the star could have been a comet or a UFO or a special creation or what have you. Of course the whole business is just a fable, a fake.

ELAINE: What do you mean?

NORMAN: I mean there wasn't any star of Bethlehem or any wise men and probably no baby in the manger either.

ELAINE: *(Indignant.)* Norman Wilson, I don't know how you can spend night after night poking that telescope into space and seeing all the things you see and still not believe in God.

NORMAN: *(Jumping up.)* Not believe in God? Who said anything about that? Of course I believe in God.

ELAINE: But you just said—

NORMAN: *(Talking down to her.)* Now look, Elaine, we've been over this before, but let's get it straight this time. I know there's a God. I just don't take any stock in the things *you* believe about him.

ELAINE: But what do you think, then?

NORMAN: I believe there's a power, a designer, a master thinker behind everything in this universe. As you so helpfully pointed out, since I spend all my time looking at the stars and planets, how could I think otherwise. Does that satisfy you?

ELAINE: Well, it sounds good to hear you say that.

NORMAN: It's certainly in line with that passage from the Bible you're always quoting at me. Something about the heavens talking about God.

ELAINE: Oh yes. The heavens *declare* the glory of God.

NORMAN: That's it. *Glory.* A good word, *glory.* This universe is a glory. That's what I see when I point the telescope at one of the distant galaxies. Glory —and mystery.

ELAINE: Mystery? To you?

NORMAN: Oh yes. We live in a tantalyzing fascinating universe, my dear. There's mystery in a comet that wanders into our solar system and then disappears. There's mystery in those distant quasars, sending out their pulses of energy. Even the rings of Saturn or the pocked surface of the moon stir me, although I've seen them a hundred times in the past few years.

ELAINE: You do enjoy your work, don't you?

NORMAN: Yes. And every time I spend an hour with that telescope I'm more convinced that whoever planned this universe is a master architect, a superb designer as well as a poet and an artist.

ELAINE: I love to hear you talk like that. I guess that's why I married you. You're such a good talker. But if you believe in God like you say you do, why are you so opposed to the church and the Bible?

NORMAN: *(Back to earth.)* Look, honey, I don't want to argue with you and say things that hurt your faith. But I just can't believe in your kind of God. When a person comes to realize the vastness of space, the billions of stars and the possibility that there may be millions of worlds like this, it doesn't make sense to talk about a God who's concerned about human individuals, about me and what I do.

ELAINE: But that's exactly what the Bible says God *is* concerned about—about you and me and what happens to us. That's what Christmas is all about —a God so concerned about us that he sent his own son to be born on this earth.

NORMAN: Well, I don't believe it. Ideas like that that were alright when men thought in terms of one little world with a few thousand people on it. But this universe is too big, too impersonal for us to expect any special care. I believe God designed everything but now it runs like a vast machine. And you and I are just tiny unimportant cogs in the whole setup.

ELAINE: I don't like being called a cog. And I think you've got the wrong picture of God and of human beings. We're his children. We're not cogs.

NORMAN: The word stung, eh? Now look, Elaine. Be reasonable. It flatters our vanity to think that there's someone up there who's concerned about us. But you and I are just two among some three or four billion human animals on this unimportant little planet. We're like microscopic amoebas in a vast ocean, like specks of dust floating in the sun's rays.

ELAINE: Is that what I am to you, an amoeba, a speck of dust?

NORMAN: Oh, for heaven's sake. Of course not, dear. But what you are to me and what you are to the maker of this universe are two different things. Do you seriously believe it makes any difference to the designer of billions of stars whether I tell a lie or tell the truth? Whether I go to church or play golf on Sunday? Whether I live or die? God's creation goes right on, whether I exist or not and he can produce billions more like me if he wants to. Look, you and Buzz are important to me and

I'm important to you. That's all there is, and that's enough.

ELAINE: But Norman—

NORMAN: Let's not discuss it any more. I did put in a rather long night at the observatory. Discussing religion can wait until some other day.

ELAINE: *(Beaten but not convinced.)* All right, dear. But I still think you've got it all wrong.

NORMAN: *(Humoring her.)* Maybe so. But leave me in my ignorance right now. Besides, I want to see Buzz. Where is he? He usually comes rushing out to see me when I get home.

ELAINE: That is strange! I wonder? Oh, I suppose he fallen asleep again. I fed him rather early and then he went back to his room to play. He probably just got tired and dozed off.

NORMAN: Well, I'm going to get him up for a few minutes. I like to see my son before I fall into bed myself for my morning nap. *(Exits.)*

ELAINE: *(Calling after him.)* Don't frighten him, dear. Wake him gently. *(Picks up paper to read.)*

NORMAN: *(Off stage.)* All right. *(Pause.)* Buzz, Buzz, where are you? Daddy's home. Buzz, are you hiding from me? Are you playing a joke on Daddy? Buzz! *(Rushing back onstage.)* Elaine, he's not there. The window in his room is wide open and there are scratches on the window sill. But Buzz isn't there!

ELAINE: Don't get so excited, dear. He never climbs out of that window. He probably just crawled under the bed and fell asleep. He couldn't have gotten out of doors. I've been in this part of the house all morning.

NORMAN: *(Still excited.)* All right. He can't be gone. But he is!

ELAINE: I guess I might as well go find him. Men are so helpless sometimes. *(Exit, but we hear her calling.)* Buzz, Buzz! Are you playing hide and seek? Buzz! Answer mama!

NORMAN: *(Searching and calling while* ELAINE *is off stage.)* Buzz, Buzz! Where are you?

ELAINE: *(Reappearing. Now she is excited.)* He isn't there, Norman! Do you suppose he *did* climb out that window? He never has.

NORMAN: There's got to be a first time for everything. I've called and called and he doesn't answer. He's not in the house!

ELAINE: Norman, do you suppose he's been kidnapped? Someone could have slipped into the house through that window and snatched him without my even knowing it. Oh, suddenly I'm afraid!

NORMAN: *(Comforting her.)* Now, Elaine, don't get panicky. Why would anyone want to kidnap him? We don't have any money for ransom.

ELAINE: No, but there are people with twisted minds in the world. Somebody might have grabbed him just on an impulse.

NORMAN: Let's not even imagine things like that unless we have to. Look, I'll go outside and scour the neighborhood and you get on the phone and call the police.

ELAINE: The police! You do think he's been kidnapped, don't you?

NORMAN: No, no. Just in case. He might have wandered off somewhere and gotten lost. Someone could have taken him to the police station. But I'm sure he's okay.

ELAINE: Norman, he's so little.

NORMAN: Take it easy. I'm on my way.
(NORMAN *exits.* ELAINE *leafs through the phone book. The phone should be on a small table. A phone on a jack, unconnected can be used. The phone bell can be recorded or a bicycle bell off stage will serve.*)

ELAINE: *(Finding the number.)* Here it is. *(Just as she reaches to pick up the phone, it rings. She grabs it.)* Hello—oh hello, Mrs. Perry. Look, I can't talk right now. Buzz has disappeared and I've got to call the police. Norman is out looking for him —what?—he is?—Having a second breakfast?—Why the little rascal—I'll be there right away—Oh, you will—Oh, fine—we'll be right here. Yes, yes—I'll have to go and tell Norman now—Goodbye. *(Puts phone down and goes to door.)* Norman, Norman, come on home. He's been found!

NORMAN: *(Off stage.)* What? What did you say?

ELAINE: *(Yelling.)* I said Buzz is okay! Come on home!

NORMAN: *(Appearing.)* Was he hiding from us? The little rascal!

ELAINE: No, he must have climbed out of the window. He went over to Mrs. Perry's house. She phoned me just when I was going to call the police.

NORMAN: Well, I'll have a word with that young man when he gets home. I'll go get him right away.

ELAINE: No, you don't need to. Mrs. Perry's bringing him back. She thought I sent him over to play and she was giving him some cookies and milk when he suddenly admitted I didn't know where he was. That's when she called me. She'll be here with him when he finishes his "second breakfast."

NORMAN: Whew. *(Moping brow.)* I'm going to sit down. Haven't had a fright like that since I had to rush you to the hospital when Buzz was born. More excitement than I bargained for so early in the morning.

ELAINE: You *were* frightened, weren't you? More than you let on?

NORMAN: I suppose I was. If anything should happen to him—

ELAINE: *(Sits down.)* Norman—

NORMAN: What, dear?

ELAINE: *(Solemnly.)* I want to ask you something.

NORMAN: Go ahead. I'll even give you money for a new dress if you want it, I feel so good right now.

ELAINE: It's not that. But why were you so excited and worried when we couldn't find Buzz? Did it make any difference?

NORMAN: What a silly question!

ELAINE: But you had just gotten through telling me that human beings are cogs, amoebas, specks of dust. Isn't Buzz that? Can't God make millions more like him?

NORMAN: Oh for Pete's sake. You never give up, do you? Look. Norman's my son. I love him. He makes my life worthwhile. He's the very image of me, as you are fond of telling me.

ELAINE: Yes, dear. But I think that has something to do with what we were arguing about. I think it says something about why God is interested in us.

NORMAN: I don't see—(*Stops and thinks. The idea dawns on him.*) Oh, I'm beginning to get it. You're saying we're not just specks of dust to God. We're his sons and he loves us.

ELAINE: Yes. I might even remind you that you were made in *his* image.

NORMAN: I'll finish your lesson for you. We're also lost and he's searching for us. (ELAINE *nods.*) Say, you didn't plan this disappearing act to show me how wrong I've been, did you?

ELAINE: No, but maybe someone else did.

NORMAN: You hit pretty hard when you hit, dear. Maybe you see more with your faith than I do with my telescope and all the instruments at the observatory.

ELAINE: I think I hear them coming. (*Both go to door.*) Come in, Mrs. Perry. Buzz, Buzz, you bad boy! (*Hugs him.*)

NORMAN: We're so grateful, Mrs. Perry. No telling where he might have gone if he hadn't come to you.

MRS. PERRY: I hope you haven't been too worried.

BUZZ: Daddy, daddy, I did it. I climbed out of the window all by myself. *(He throws himself into his father's arms.* NORMAN *picks him up.)*

NORMAN: *(Hugging him.)* Yes, Buzz, you did it. But you mustn't do it again. Your mama was worried. And I was worried. And even—even God was worried. But you're safe now. Safe with those who love you. And so am I, thank God.

Incredible but True

Text: Luke 15:4-7

Christianity is incredible. It involves truths so strange and so overwhelming that the mind of man is set whirling. Most of us have heard "the old old story" so many times that we have lost our sense of wonder at Christian truth. But suppose for a moment that you had never heard the gospel. Listen for the strange and wondrous notes in the message. This is what we believe.

We believe in a God who is personally concerned about human beings, a God who made and sustains this vast universe and yet who is still interested in the welfare of individuals on this small planet. The picture takes your breath away. J. B. Phillips may be right when he says in a book title, *Your God Is Too Small* but it takes a big picture of God to fill the Christian vision.

Modern science has vastly increased the gap between God and his creatures but even the men in the Old Testament grasped the strangeness of God's interest in man. Isaiah 40 says about God: "It is he who sits above the circle of the earth and its inhabitants are like grasshoppers; who stretches out the heavens like a curtain, and spreads them like a tent to dwell in." The writer of the eighth Psalm looks at the sky and then at man and declares: "When I look at thy heavens, the work of thy fingers, the moon and the stars which thou hast established; what is man that thou art mindful of him, and the son of man that thou dost care for him?" But perhaps the best vision of this gap between God and man as well as the most humiliating passage in all literature is found in the Book of Job beginning with Chapter 38 where God challenges Job to compare his wisdom with God's. Anytime you feel too pleased with your own importance, sit down and read that section of the Bible. Yet Christianity says God is interested and concerned about man. Incredible.

Moreover Christian faith does not allow any elitism, any favoritism. We do not believe that God is interested in *some* men. We do not say that some people are so good, so noble that it is only natural that God would be interested in their welfare. That might make a very rational view. But Christian faith says *all* men. God loves the world. He is concerned about the blind beggar, the staggering alcoholic, the little child, about the black man, the white man, the rich and the poor.

How vividly the parable of the lost sheep portrays this fact and yet how far it falls short of reality. Ninety-nine sheep safe but the shepherd is still concerned about the one who is lost. That's God, only he has close to four billion sheep in this present world and who knows how many billions before our time and how many will still be born. And God loves them all. Incredible. Marvelous but incredible.

But Christian faith goes beyond this. It says that God came seeking man, that the Son left his place as ruler of all things, took on humanity, was actually born as a human being. Christian faith says that God's love was so great that he was willing to lie in a manger, to subject himself to the discipline of a human family, to take on the limitations of human flesh, yes even to suffer and die for mankind.

God then is like this shepherd in the parable, walking over wild moors, clambering over rocks, stretching out his arms to rescue a wandering sheep from destruction. Thus God is not only concerned but actively concerned about man. A number of years ago a prominent Jewish theologian, seeking to ascertain what was original about the message of Jesus, centered his attention on this parable of the lost sheep because it presents God as a seeking God. This, he declared was the unique and new truth that Jesus brought.

Perhaps this is why Christmas has had a fascination for the church, why the birth of Christ has been celebrated. After all it is only the beginning of a story that rises to its climax at a cross and an empty tomb. Yet the events of Christmas are so incredible, so stunning in their implication—God coming to rescue man. The Babe in the manger is a perfect witness of the nature of God, a God so concerned that he has come to this small planet to save his children.

But we must take one last step. This picture of God becomes most overwhelming when we make it personal. The gospel says God so loved you, so loved me that he came for us. Now do a bit of introspec-

tion, of inward reflection. Think of your life, honestly and clearly. Do you deserve such love? Are you
worthy of God's consideration? Can you say, I deserve it? God owes it to me? Or must you echo Isaac
Watts, "Amazing pity, grace unknown, and love beyond degree." When we see ourselves as the lost
sheep whom God came to rescue, the Christian message becomes truly incredible.

And yet—true. Incredible but true. That's the marvelous part of it all. Christianity is no fairy story,
spun out of some man's fertile imagination. For the
sheep was rescued by the shepherd and since Jesus
told this story millions of people have experienced
the power of God in their lives.

Sometimes we grow discouraged in our faith and
feel that Christianity is all an illusion, all a dream.
When that happens, we need to think of the people
who have experienced exactly what is described in
this parable—the joy of being saved by God. We
think of Paul and Augustine and Luther and Wesley
and all the great leaders in the church. But we also
need to include that great multitude pictured in
Revelation 7, people from every nation, from all
tribes and peoples and tongues standing before the
throne of God. Christianity may seem incredible but
its truth is witnessed in the lives of millions who
have been saved by a seeking God.

The parable of the lost sheep may seem a strange
text for Christmas. But actually, the whole story of
Jesus is mirrored in these four verses from the Gospel
of Luke. For Christmas is God, come to seek his lost
sheep. Christmas is love demonstrated in action.
Christmas is rescue and joy. Christmas is incredible
but true.

The Patient Farmer

Mark 4:26-29
EPIPHANY OR NEW YEAR

DRAMA	**What's the Verdict?**
MEDITATION	**God's Time — and Ours**

What's the Verdict?

Based on Mark 4:26-29. The parable should not be read before the play as it is read during the production.

CHARACTERS

JUDGE JOHN KELLEY: fairly young; should have a strong voice

BAILIFF: can be either a man or a woman

MRS. PURVIS: not too old; a widow

NICK WILSON: teen-ager or early twenties

MISS CARTER: middle-aged; not very healthy looking

REV. THOMPSON: fairly young clergyman

STRANGER: no particular age; dominates scene at end

SETTING

A courtroom setting with judge's seat at one end and the chairs facing the judge. Witness stand should face audience directly.

COSTUMES

Contemporary. Judge needs a black robe. Clergyman should wear a clerical if possible.

(The opening and closing speeches of JUDGE KELLEY should be made in front of the courtroom scene. If there is a curtain, it should be closed at the outset or lights can be switched on for courtroom. At least there should be an indication of scene change here though it can be done very simply by a change of position.)

JUDGE: *(Walking onstage.)* Good evening, ladies and gentlemen. My name is John Kelley. I'm the judge of the municipal court in this city. No, I'm not here seeking votes. I simply want to share with you an experience that I had recently. Actually it was a dream, but it seemed so strange and yet so realistic that I find it hard to think of it as a dream. As I said, my work is to preside over the municipal court. So everyday I see people who are involved in crimes, disputes, ugliness, and all the troubles that human beings face or cause. The key to my work can be summed up in one word—unhappiness.

When I go home I try to put all this behind me. A man can't think about unpleasant things all the time without getting terribly depressed. So at home I seldom talk about my work, seldom even think about it. And I never dream about it. That's why this experience the other night was so strange. I dreamed I was back in my courtroom with my bailiff and outside there was a noisy mob, trying to get in the door. Here, let me put on my robe (Dons black robe which was lying on chair) and I'll show you what happened. Please remember that all this is a dream, a figment of my imagination. (JUDGE *sits on chair in courtroom scene with* BAILIFF *close to him. Crowd noises and pounding on door.)* Bailiff, bailiff, what's going on outside there? What's all the noise about?

BAILIFF: Oh your honor, it's a crazy mob of people. They keep yelling that they want justice and I think they'll break the door down if we don't do something.

JUDGE: Well, this is a court of justice. Open the door and let them in.

BAILIFF: Let that mob in here, sir! Why they might attack or even kill you. Mobs don't stop to think what they're doing.

JUDGE: I think I can handle a small mob. Let them in.

BAILIFF: Well, don't say I didn't warn you. *(Opens door.* MRS. PURVIS, NICK, MISS CARTER, *and* REV. THOMPSON *head for the judge. Others may be added to mob if desired but they stay in background. The* STRANGER *sits down and calmly begins to read a newspaper. The four leaders yell* We want justice! We've been tricked! You've got to help us! *as they face the judge. Then they begin to chant in unison,* We want justice!)

JUDGE: *(Pounding for order.)* Quiet, quiet. This is a court of law, not a football stadium.

MRS. PURVIS: But we want justice.

JUDGE: You'll get more justice than you bargained for if you don't sit down and be quiet. *(They take their places, mumbling.)* That's better. Now, what's this all about? *(The four all stand up and begin to talk at once.)* One at a time. You there *(Indicat-*

ing Mrs. Purvis) tell me what's troubling you.
And the rest of you sit down. *(They do so.)* Well?

Mrs. Purvis: *(Standing.)* I'm asking a judgment, your
honor, for breach of contract.

Judge: I see. And who are you suing for this breach?
Someone in the courtroom?

Mrs. Purvis: No sir. I'm suing *God!*

Judge: God? Merciful heavens. *(Recovering self.)* I
see. Well, we'll get to your case in a few minutes,
ma'am.

Mrs. Purvis: Thank you. *(Sits down.)*

Judge: *(To* Bailiff) Watch her, Bailiff. She's a nut.
Don't take your eyes off of her. *(To group.)* Let's
see what some of the rest of you have to complain
about. You, young man. *(To* Nick.) What's your
trouble?

Nick: It's very simple, sir. I don't have exactly the
same complaint as the lady there but I also want
to sue God for breach of contract.

Judge: Oh no! *(Motions to* Nick *to sit down, which
he does.)* Bailiff, watch him. He's another one.
Don't take your eyes off him.

Bailiff: But how can I? I've got to watch that woman.

Judge: Do as I say.

Bailiff: Yes sir. *(Keeps head moving back and
forth.)*

Judge: *(To* Miss Carter.) Now you, ma'am. Are you
also here to sue God?

MISS CARTER: *(Bobbing up and down.)* Yes, your honor.

JUDGE: Bailiff, bailiff!

BAILIFF: I know. Watch her too. *(Nervous motions from one to another.)*

JUDGE: I think you people have made a mistake. This is a court of law, not a church. But I see a clergyman present. Pastor, Reverend, Father, whatever you call yourself, can't you help these people?

THOMPSON: But your honor, I'm asking for a judgment against God just like the others are.

JUDGE: Now I've heard everything. Look, I can't deal with a dispute like this. I can't bring God into court or fine him or even question him. I can do nothing for you here.

(The four and perhaps others leave their seats and advance on JUDGE *yelling and complaining as before.* JUDGE *pounds for order.)* All right, all right. Sit down and be quiet.

MISS CARTER: Will you give us a hearing?

JUDGE: Yes, I'll hear you. *(They take their places again.)* Maybe if you state your complaints, that'll make you feel better. But you'll have to recognize that I have no power to help you even if you should win your cases. You understand that?

THOMPSON: We understand, your honor.

JUDGE: All right. I'll take you one at a time. You, madam. *(To* MRS. PURVIS.*)* I might as well start with you. You're no crazier than the rest. *(She moves to witness stand, facing audience.)*

BAILIFF: Shall I swear the witness?

JUDGE: What good would that do? She's suing God. (BAILIFF *goes back in disgust.*) Now, your name please?

MRS. PURVIS: Mrs. Mary Purvis.

JUDGE: You're married, then?

MRS. PURVIS: I'm a widow, sir.

JUDGE: I see. State your case.

MRS. PURVIS: I'm a Christian, your honor. At least I thought I was until recently. Rev. Thompson can tell you I've always been a faithful church member.

THOMPSON: (*Standing up.*) I can vouch for that, sir. (*Sits.*)

JUDGE: All right, Mrs. Purvis. We'll take your word for it. But accusing God of breach of contract doesn't sound very Christian to me.

MRS. PURVIS: I can't help it. You see, two years ago my husband died. And that started it all.

JUDGE: Oh come now, Mrs. Purvis. You can't blame God for that. People die all the time. God didn't promise that any of us would live forever.

MRS. PURVIS: I know that. I'm not blaming God that my husband died. But your honor, are you familiar with the sermon on the mount?

JUDGE: Yes. What's that got to do with it?

MRS. PURVIS: Let me read one verse to you. (*Opens Bible which she had in pocket or handbag.*) Here it is. "Blessed are they that mourn for they shall be comforted (Matt. 5:4). Your honor, is that a promise or not?

JUDGE: Why—I suppose it is.

MRS. PURVIS: And wouldn't you consider two years a reasonable length of time for a person to wait for someone to keep a promise?

JUDGE: Sounds like that should be sufficient.

MRS. PURVIS: Well, God hasn't kept his word. I haven't found any comfort in the past two years. I loved my husband and I still miss him terribly. When I wake up in the morning, he's not there beside me. When I sit down at the breakfast table there's an empty chair opposite me. When evening comes and he should be coming home from work, I listen for his step and the sound of his key in the door but there's only silence. The whole house is filled with memories of him.

JUDGE: But there's your trouble, Mrs. Purvis. You ought to get away from that house.

MRS. PURVIS: I tried that. I leased my house and even moved out of town. It didn't make any difference. The loneliness was still there. No comfort, no comfort anywhere.

JUDGE: Have you tried working, keeping busy, helping others who are in trouble? That often takes people's minds off their grief.

MRS. PURVIS: I've tried everything. I've prayed, I've read my Bible, I've gone to church, I've done charitable deeds. And still no comfort. I tell you, God has deceived me. *(Getting louder.)* He promised to help me but he hasn't. I say he's in breach of contract and I want a judgment against him.

JUDGE: Thank you, Mrs. Purvis. I'll take your case under advisement. But perhaps you'll step down now and let me hear some of the others. *(She steps down.* JUDGE *to* BAILIFF.*)* A very sad case, Bailiff.

BAILIFF: Very sad indeed. Glad you have to deal with it and not me.

JUDGE: Thanks a lot. *(To* NICK.*)* Young man, suppose you come and state your difficulty.

NICK: Yes , sir. *(Takes witness chair.)* My name is Nick Wilson. And I guess I'd better begin by reading this verse from James. *(Takes out New Testament and reads James 1:5.)* "If any of you lacks wisdom, let him ask God, who gives to all men generously and without reproaching and it will be given him." There's my complaint, your honor.

JUDGE: Can you be more specific?

NICK: Yes sir. You see, I'm not very smart. I don't mean that I can't do my school work or learn things. But I get into trouble with other people.

JUDGE: What kind of trouble?

NICK: Just—trouble. At home I seem to say the wrong things. I get my father mad at me and make my mother cry. And I don't intend to at all. Then I pick people to be my friends and they turn out to be bad ones. One fellow got me to steal and a girl almost got me hooked on drugs.

JUDGE: That's bad, young man.

NICK: I know it, sir. I sure seem to fit that description of a fellow who lacks wisdom. A year or so ago I read this promise in James and thought that was the answer. So I started to pray and ask God for help, just like the Bible says.

JUDGE: Nick, have you tried to help yourself? You can't expect God to do all the work.

NICK: I *have* tried, Judge. And I've prayed and prayed. Sometimes it seems like I'm making a little progress but I still do stupid things. Yesterday I got so angry at my sister that I hit her. And that was the end of it. My prayers aren't doing any good. God hasn't given me any wisdom. I've been deceived and I want judgment against God, judgment, judgment. *(Loud at end.)*

JUDGE: Well, you seem to have a case. But now, suppose you step down and let this lady tell her story. *(Indicates* MISS CARTER.*)* She seems to have a complaint too.

NICK: Yes, your honor. *(Takes his seat.)*

JUDGE: Step up, ma'am. (MISS CARTER *comes slowly up the aisle.)*

MISS CARTER: Thank you, Judge. I have to walk a bit slow because my heart isn't too good.

JUDGE: I'm sorry.

MISS CARTER: Oh, I've learned to live with that and a lot of other things. *(Sits in chair.)*

JUDGE: You are?

MISS CARTER: Miss Jane Carter. I guess my complaint is like the others. I've had a lot of trouble in my lifetime.

JUDGE: So have many other people, Miss Carter. I hear people tell about their troubles every day in this courtroom

MISS CARTER: I'm sure you do, sir. But it's not the trouble that bothers me. It's the uselessness of it all.

JUDGE: I don't understand.

MISS CARTER: Well, your honor, I've spent a good part of my life in and out of hospitals. Seems like when I get over one illness, another comes along. Never was able to work regularly. Never had a boyfriend because I was too sickly to go places where other young people went. But I've come to accept all that. I don't want you to think I'm just a complainer. At least I've tried not to be.

JUDGE: I see. But you are complaining that God has allowed you to suffer more than other people. Isn't that so?

MISS CARTER: Oh no. But God promises that everything works together for good for those that love him. And I've believed that all these years. Every time some new trouble came along, I said to myself, "Jane Carter, some good will come out of this. Just keep on trusting." And then last week I lost my job again because I was sick. And that made me sit down and think.

JUDGE: The straw that broke the camel's back?

MISS CARTER: I guess so. I decided that I'd been

fooled all these years. Things hadn't worked out for good. Nothing had turned out right. Nothing. And I said to myself, "Jane Carter, you've been a fool. God's been playing games with you. And that's not right. It's not honest. I've been mistreated." So I want judgment for all my years of pain and trouble. I want justice, your honor.

JUDGE: You have my sympathy, Miss. But now suppose we let the clergyman tell his story. Then I'll try to come to some kind of verdict for all of you.

MISS CARTER: Thank you, your honor. (*Steps down and goes to seat.*)

JUDGE: (*Indicating* THOMPSON.) Come here, sir. I'm a bit surprised to see you in this company.

THOMPSON: (*Taking witness chair.*) I'm surprised to be here. But in all honesty I felt I had to add my complaints to the others.

JUDGE: And what's your trouble? Haven't your parishioners been paying your salary? Or have the old ladies of the parish gotten on your nerves?

THOMPSON: Nothing like that, your honor. It's just that suddenly I feel all my hopes have been shattered. All my life I've looked forward to one great event—the return of Jesus Christ. I've studied what the Bible has to say, I've read books about it, I've preached dozens of sermons on the subject.

JUDGE: Your problem is theological, is it?

THOMPSON: Partly, I suppose. I've believed and I've told my people that at any moment the Lord might be in their midst. Then last Sunday when

I was preaching the same thing again, a man stood up in church and said, "Nonsense. He hasn't come and he's not coming."

JUDGE: That must have given you a start.

THOMPSON: More than that. It made me think. It reminds me of all the other ministers before me who had preached the same message and nothing had happened. And suddenly I decided that I had been misleading myself and everybody else. The Lord wasn't coming at all. I felt that God had fooled me, just as he had the others who've testified in this court today.

JUDGE: That's a terrible thing for a clergyman to say.

THOMPSON: I know, I know. *(Buries head in hands for a moment.)* But I can't help feeling that God makes promises and doesn't keep them, that he's guilty of a breach of contract with men. And I think you as a judge ought to decide that we are right in our complaints. That won't change things much but at least we'll feel that we have right on our side. That's all, your honor. *(Bows head and walks back to his seat.)*

JUDGE: Well, we've heard the complaints. You've given me a hard task. But before I render a decision, is there anyone here who wants to say a word in defense of God? Any spokesman for the defense in this case?

STRANGER: *(Has been reading newspaper during entire play.)* I would like to speak, your honor.

JUDGE: You? Who are you?

STRANGER: *(Walking to front.)* My name's not important. But I would like to read a few words to the court. Words from that same book the others have been quoting.

JUDGE: Why not? Everything else is strange about this case.

STRANGER: Thank you. The words are these: "The kingdom of God is as if a man should scatter seed upon the ground and should sleep and rise night and day, and the seed should sprout and grow, he knows not how. The earth produces of itself, first the blade, then the ear, then the full grain in the ear. But when the grain is ripe, at once he puts in the sickle, because the harvest has come" (Mark 4:26-29). Your honor, I move that you find in favor of God in this case.

MISS CARTER: Wait a minute.

NICK: I don't get it.

STRANGER: It's very simple. Time is in God's hands, not ours. He gives comfort and wisdom and meaning to life when he is ready. And our Lord will return when the harvest is ripe, not before. I appeal to you, your honor. Decide for God, not for men.

MRS. PURVIS: No, no.

THOMPSON: Is there no end to the waiting?

JUDGE: *(Pounds gavel.)* Quiet everyone. I've had enough of this. I give my verdict in favor of—*(The curtain is drawn, lights lowered, or the characters freeze and the* JUDGE *steps to his original position at the front of the stage.)* I woke up at that moment. I was in a cold bedroom but I was fevered and soaked in perspiration. And all that remained was a big question mark. How had I decided? What was the right decision? Were these worried and disturbed people, these figures in my dream, right or wrong in their complaints?

Well, now I've told you my dream. So maybe I can pass the decision on to you. How would you have decided if you had been the judge? What would your verdict have been? I put the matter in your hands. And now, good evening, Pleasant dreams.

God's Time—and Ours

Text: Mark 4:26-29

Time. Time is a very strange thing. St. Augustine in his *Confessions* says he knows what it is if no one asks him to define it. Most of us probably feel that way too. We all know how to measure time, of course. We slice it into days and hours and minutes and seconds; indeed scientists can even divide the seconds into infinitesimally small segments. But we are aware that such divisions are artificial and sometimes misleading.

Thus sixty minutes listening to a boring lecture just isn't the same as an hour spent with someone we love, no matter what the clock says. Twenty-four hours of leisure in the country isn't the same as a day spent racing to and fro in the city. Time is relative and comparisons are therefore very difficult.

When we add God's time to the picture, we really begin to face problems. Almost immediately we remember the explanation in Second Peter that in God's sight a thousand years is as a day and a day as a thousand years. That can really mix us up but it does throw some light on our text which deals with the slow patient waiting until harvest. Certainly we must agree that God operates on a different time schedule than we do.

But this difference is extremely important. Many of our difficulties with God arise because of this difference in viewpoint. We want instant action. God seems slow and deliberate in his ways. We are like the small boy who plants a seed today and digs it up tomorrow to see if it is growing. God takes four hundred years to rescue his people from Egypt. No wonder we often feel disappointed and let down by God.

Perhaps the most striking example of this difference in time occurred in the appearance of Jesus on this earth. Man from the beginning looked for a redeemer, a savior to rescue him from his difficulties. Some have thought that when Eve declared: "I have gotten a man with the help of the Lord," Gen. 4:1b she imagined that the rescuer from God had arrived. The child turned out to be Cain. Regardless of how we interpret Eve's words, there can be no doubt that the prophets of the Old Testament were always crying for help and telling God that the time for him to fulfill his promises had come. Yet God operated on his own time schedule. Only when the fulness of time had come, only when the harvest was ripe did God send the Christ.

The same difference in time occurs in our world today. We all grow impatient for God to act. We want him to solve our problems, heal our bodies, bring peace among nations. We can all sympathize with the woman who saw her husband dying inch

by inch and cried out: "God, why are you so slow?"
And yet the reality which we must face is that God
works on a different schedule.

Perhaps it isn't too hard to see why this is true.
Note that the parable speaks of seed growing to harvest. The farmer is concerned about the end result.
He knows what his goal is and he takes no action
until everything is *ripe* for action. So God is always
aware of the goal, the end. He knew when to send
the Savior because he knew what he wanted to ac-
complish. And he is concerned about final results,
about his goal in our lives.

Of course we are too, but we can never quite
grasp what the final result will be. We often think
only in terms of this world; God also has eternity in
focus. We cry out in pain without any real grasp of
what the pain may be for. It is like the parent who
takes his son to have his tonsils removed. The child
sees only the strange doctor and the unfamiliar sur-
roundings; the parent sees a child stronger and more
healthy as a result of the operation.

This doesn't mean that it is sinful to complain.
God didn't rebuke the prophets because they were
eager for deliverance to come. Job was vindicated,
despite his cries against the suffering that he had to
endure. And God knows our weakness and our blind-
ness too. After all, he is aware that his time is different from ours. When troubles come, it is natural for
us to cry out. Only step by step we must learn to
rely on God and put our trust in his greater wisdom.

For God's time to act always comes, and his action
is always successful. Note that there is no question
raised in the text about the harvest. The seed ripens
into grain. It does not fail. And God's plans do not

fail either. He may take more time than we think he should but God always makes good on his promises.

The coming of Jesus into the world is the most striking example of our text. God's plans cover the entire Old Testament period. The time lapse from Abraham to Christ is about the same as from Christ to our present age. Think of all that could have gone wrong in that length of time. Think of all that did go wrong. Yet the seed came to the harvest.

It is this that gives the Christian confidence. We don't face an iffy situation when we put our trust in God. We're dealing with a reputable firm. God brings his plans to harvest. This is the message of that last book of the Bible, the book of Revelation. Filled as it is with peculiar and bizarre figures, the book repeats again and again assurance that God will win. In fact in the fourteenth chapter the figure of the sickle and the harvest is again used to express the completeness of God's victory.

In this Epiphany season, we are once more celebrating the appearance of our Lord on this earth. We usually think of this appearance in its relationship to our salvation and of course that is a proper understanding of Epiphany. But perhaps it should also be seen as a witness for all time of how God operates. He sent his son into the world when he was ready. He redeemed his promise as he always does. Isaac Watts said it very well when he wrote:

O God our help in ages past, our hope for years to come,
Our shelter from the stormy blast, and our eternal home:
Under the shadow of thy throne thy saints have dwelt secure;
Sufficient is thine arm alone, and our defence is sure.